D1245492

BROTHER ENEMY

BROTHER ENEMY

POEMS OF THE KOREAN WAR

■

**Translated by
SUH JI-MOON**

■

**In Collaboration With
JAMES A. PERKINS**

■

WHITE PINE PRESS   ■   **BUFFALO, NEW YORK**

Grand Forks Public Library

Copyright ©2002 by Suh Ji-moon
Translations copyright ©2002 by Suh Ji-moon

All rights reserved. This work, or portions thereof,
may not be reproduced in any form without permission.

Publication of this book was made possible by grants from
The Korea Literature Translation Institute
and the New York State Council on the Arts.

Book design: Elaine LaMattina

Printed and bound in the United States of America

ISBN 1-893996-20-4

First Edition

Library of Congress Control Number:: 2002106766

Published by
White Pine Press
P.O. Box 236, Buffalo, New York 14201

www.whitepine.org

■ CONTENTS

Introduction by Suh Ji-moon - 11

Cho Chi-hun, from *Before the Tribunal of History*
Journal of Despair   (June 25, 1950) - 39
Journal of Despair   (June 26, 1950) - 40
Journal of Despair   (June, 27 1950) - 42
Journal of Despair   (June 28, 1950) - 45
A Pledge - 46
Return Victorious! - 47
Written from the Combat Front - 49
Romantic Army Life - 50
At Ch'ŏngma's Temporary Residence - 51
At Tabuwon - 52
At Toriwon - 54
Here Lies a Communist Soldier - 55
The Battle of Chukryŏng Pass - 57
On Returning to Seoul - 58
At a Tavern in Pongilch'ŏn - 61
You Are Crossing the Thirty-Eighth Parallel - 62
A Farmer's Hut in Yŏnbaek - 63
Heartless Taedong River - 64
Poetry on the Wall - 65
At Chongro - 66

Yu Ch'i-hwan, from *With the Foot Soldier*
With the Simplicity of a Child - 71
Like a Wildflower - 72
At the Front Line - 73
Beautiful Soldiers - 74
A Short Rest - 75
To My Daughter, Yŏng-a - 76
Diamond Mountain - 77
The Search Squadron - 78

The Meaning of Flags - 79
Forward March - 80
Cowardice - 81
To Comrades - 82
Life and Death - 83
Like a Red Peony - 84
I Ask You - 85
Fleeing the War - 86
Resolution - 87
To the East Sea - 88
To a Deceased United Nations Soldier - 89
Port of Glory - 90
Glory Be to the Dutch Flag Forever - 91
Cleansing a Territory with the Enemy's Blood - 92
A Counteroffensive - 93
Reeds - 94
At Christmas 1950 - 95
Drifters - 96
Where to Go? - 97
My Fatherland - 98
At the Combat Front - 99
At the Armistice Line - 101

Ku Sang, from *Poetry on Burnt Ground*

Poetry on Burnt Ground 1 - 105
Poetry on Burnt Ground 2 - 105
Poetry on Burnt Ground 3 - 106
Poetry on Burnt Ground 4 - 107
Poetry on Burnt Ground 7 - 108
Poetry on Burnt Ground 8 - 109
Poetry on Burnt Ground 9 - 110
Poetry on Burnt Ground 10 - 111

Yu Ch'un-do, from *Unforgettable People*

Destiny - 115
"I Love You, Comrade" - 116
The Girl Soldier and the Moon - 118
The Emergency Field Hospital - 120
Maggots - 122
Namgang River - 123
Kŭmgang River Ghost - 124
Let's Take Our Own Lives - 125
In Ch'ŏngju Prison - 127
Crickets Chirping in My Ear - 130
The Female Guerrilla - 131

Mo Yun-suk

What the Dead Soldier Said - 135

Chang Ho-gang

A Hymn to a Comrade - 141
If I Fall - 143
Kansas Line - 144
The Armistice Line at Night - 146
Dedicating a Flower - 148

Chang Su-ch'ŏl

In the Freezing Trench - 151

Kim Kwang-rim

April, Which Prepared for June - 155

Kim Kyu-dong

A Grave - 159

Min J'ae-shik

Scapegoats - 163

Mun Sang-myŏng
>   White Horse Hill - 167
>   Lost Time and Effaced Language - 169
>   The Blackout Line - 170

Pak Il-song
>   War Diary - 177
>   The Eyes of the Sentry - 179

Pak In-hwan
>   To My Baby Daughter - 183

Pak Pong-u
>   Blooming on the Wasteland - 187
>   The Window - 189
>   Half-Moon - 191
>   The Armistice Line - 192

Pak Yang-kyun
>   Flower - 195

Yi Hyo-sang
>   Fatherland - 199
>   War - 200

Yi Yong-sang
>   The Day You Tearfully Embrace Our Fatherland - 203
>   I Can Love a North Korean - 204

Yi Tŏk-chin
>   The Ridge of Blood - 209

Yi Yun-su
>   The Foot Soldier Marches - 213
>   The Northern Front - 215

Yu Chŏng

      Envy - 219
      Brothers - 220

Syngman Rhee

      At Pulguksa Temple - 223
      Swallow - 224
      On the Road Between Chinhae and Pusan - 225
      Spring in Wartime - 226
      A Casual Verse - 227
      At Haein Temple - 228
      At the Ch'ŏnggan Pavilion in Kansong - 229

Notes on the Poems - 230

Introduction
by Suh Ji-moon
■

The Korean War started with a surprise attack launched by North Korea at dawn on the 25th of June, 1950. Although South Korea was quite unprepared for the invasion that shattered the peace of a bright Sunday morning, it wasn't wholly unexpected. The mood of hostility between the Communist-controlled north and the U.S.-bolstered south had been such that disaster hung in the air. "I knew this was bound to happen./ And it has come at last" poet Cho Chi-hun says in "Journal of Despair, June 25, 1950."

The fact that it was to some degree foreseen didn't make the war more bearable. It was, in fact, the worst calamity to happen to a country whose "only constant companion/ Has been calamity" (Ku Sang, "Poetry on Burnt Ground"). War is always a disaster and a tragedy for everyone involved, but the fact that the enemy was not some foreign devil but fellow countrymen—often a cousin or brother—made it a horror beyond conception and description. The inhabitants of the northern and the southern halves of Korea harbored a strong regional prejudice against each other—as is usual in many countries of the world—but there was no clear regional or even class demarcation between the adherents of liberal democracy and of communism in post-liberation Korea. From the commencement of the Communist dominion in the north, a deluge of North Koreans—estimated at over one million, most of them former landlords, intellectuals, or Christians—fled south to escape persecution. A fraction of that number of South Koreans—mostly intellectuals, many of them from the privileged class—migrated north in search of an ideological haven. That does not mean that the majority of people who stayed put did so out of ideological sympathy for their respective regimes. Most were ideological innocents whose strong local interests or ties kept them from seeking new lives in strange places.

North Korean troops, therefore, did not consist only of Communist followers, nor were the South Korean soldiers all liberal democrats. Many young men were conscripted into either the South or North Korean army simply by reason of their residence in the respective region. In addition, many South Korean youths (and mere lads) "volunteered" to fight in the North Korean "Righteous and Valiant Army" because they were unable to flee before the Communists took over their region in the early days of the war. Similarly, North Korean youths were inducted into the South Korean army while South Korea occupied the North, from October to December of 1950. Therefore, brother, uncle and nephew, even father and son fighting on opposite sides—some from conviction, and many from compulsion—were not at all uncommon. Many such volunteers were pulled right out of paddies and fishing boats and thrown onto battlefields with only a few days'—sometimes only a few hours'—military training. Though both sides suffered from a lack of supplies throughout the war, there was never any shortage of tragic irony on either side.

Therefore, unlike at the beginning of the First World War, there was little sense of rallying around the banner of justice and fighting a war to make the world safer and more free. Rather, there was a fratricidal guilt similar to that which preyed on the hearts of some American Civil War poets. The fact that Koreans were very proud of their national homogeneity, believing themselves to be common descendants of Tangun, Korea's legendary founder and original father-king, intensified these feelings.

When the Korean War broke out, the South Korean Defense Ministry called in writers to produce morale-raising propaganda. But at the beginning of the war, the South Korean army suffered one shattering defeat after another and was pushed all the way down to the Naktong River. It was only after the North Korean advance was checked at the Pusan perimeter that the Defense Ministry could organize writers and poets into an effective auxiliary unit. However, since the Defense Ministry had the responsibility of running the war on many fronts, the writers were not always properly regimented and cared for. Not only did they suffer physical discomfort, but their very lives were often imperiled.

Perhaps the writers, required to write without any security in their own lives, stayed on partly because they dreaded the consequences of escape or desertion. But I believe they also stayed out of a sense of patriotic duty. Some critics from the generation born a decade and more after the war brand these writers as "Ŏyong," writers in the government's pay. This is not only a great injustice to the writers but a calumny cast on all who resisted the Communist aggression and survived it. And the poems these poets wrote are far from patriotic in the common sense. Most of the poems by the major poets included in this collection, except for a handful of poems praising the valor of ROK soldiers and denouncing the inhuman cruelty of the Communists, are suffused with pain and sadness in the face of the devastation wrought by the war and express the futility of a war in which victory means death and injury for the other half of one's own nation. A number of poems openly express compassion for, and sorrow over, the enemy dead—enemy who might be one's own brother. It must have taken a lot of courage to write such poems while acting as the "official" poets of the Republic of Korea. A number of poems in this anthology made me wonder if they didn't get their authors in trouble with the military authorities.

Unfortunately, most of the poems that were written under such perilous circumstances have been buried in oblivion. It was difficult to unearth the poems for the 1999 Mansfield-Center-organized Dialogue on the Korean War, and for this anthology. I suspect that the main reason for their dropping out of circulation is that Koreans in the 1950s and 1960s were too devastated by the war and the struggle for survival during those indigent times to enjoy poems recalling the horrors and sorrows of war. The repressive character of successive regimes put patriotic literature out of favor with literary critics. Also, the poems are extremely spare and do not display the techniques contemporary readers look for in poetry.

Whatever the reasons for their neglect, the Korean War poems I discovered moved me profoundly. The most important finds were *Before the Tribunal of History* by Cho Chi-hun and *With the Foot Soldier* by Yu Ch'i-hwan. Though no longer in print, these volumes are not hard to find. Ku Sang's *Poetry on Burnt Ground*, written from the rear of the battlefront during the war, is also easily found, but I had to glean most of the other poems in this collection from dusty library shelves or with the help of senior scholars. Yu Ch'un-do's *Unforgettable People*, the 1999 collection that deals with her experiences as an army doctor to the North Koreans, was a most welcome and timely find. The poems of this successful medical doctor, wife and mother who has lived with her nightmare for half a century forcibly brought home to me once again all the tragic paradoxes of the Korean War. Syngman Rhee's poems, written in Chinese, were interesting and valuable more for their literary qualities than as political statements of the South Korean president responsible for the safety and survival of twenty million people. We cannot infer from the poems what kind of a president Dr. Rhee was, but they testify that he was a very good poet in the classic Chinese tradition.

Because most of the poems employ very few of the techniques contemporary poets are fond of utilizing—deliberate ambiguity, pointed irony, verbal fireworks—and instead are very stark and spare, they read like poems from another era. At first glance they may look unsophisticated, but I felt the presence of a major poet in the extreme simplicity of Yu Ch'i-hwan's and Cho Chi-hun's poems. And most of the poems inspired in me the awe that only the most authentic emotion in the face of tragic and harrowing experience can inspire.

The works of the lesser-known poets lacked the sure touch of the major poets and were of uneven quality, but they moved me in another way. Many of them were written by actual soldiers and gave me a picture of what went on in the battlefield and in the soldiers' minds. About half the poets are poets of considerable note; the rest are now almost totally forgotten, and because of the postwar social turmoil, even their biographical facts are not easy to ascertain. I was doubly glad to discover them and to bring them to light once more.

As a literary critic I am aware that a number of the poems in this collection are unsophisticated in terms of literary technique. Yet most of them gave me the kind of emotional experience only great literature can give—a sense of frail human beings rising to meet the tyrannies and cruelties of life with dignity and with humility. It was a profoundly painful experience, yet it gave me at the same time a solemn and chastened kind of elation.

*   *   *

Cho Chi-hun, scion of a family of Confucian scholars, was a poet and a professor of Korean literature at the time of the outbreak of the Korean War. Poetically, he was an aesthete tempered by Confucian self-discipline and Buddhist spirituality, and his poems are generally graceful meditations on objects that inspire a sense of spiritual beauty and nobility. His integrity and the ascetic quality of his work are evident in many of his Korean War poems, though not much of his exquisite aesthetic sensibility is. The day after the Korean War broke out, when most people were terrified but still clinging to the government's assurance that there would be no difficulty in defending the capital, students came to class but couldn't concentrate on the lecture. Cho, their professor, observes:

> Two o'clock in the afternoon
> I give a lecture on poetics in a third-floor classroom of Korea University.
> I hear the noise of guns from the direction of Ŭijŏngbu.

The loudspeaker on campus tremulously relays news from the battlefront.

Youths seem to regard poetry as irrelevant to the moment.
But it is at moments of crises that poetry can be our support.

"Now you'll realize the meaning of the anxiety of being,"
I tell them.

. . . .

Pushing the door open and coming out into the hallway,
I see poetry sucked away by the smoke of battle.

("Journal of Despair, Twenty-sixth of June, 1950")

"At Toriwon" describes the ruins of a village that was the site of one of the fiercest and most atrocious battles in the war's early stages. The poem's quiet sorrow, which might look like detachment to a careless reader, actually hides profound sorrow and even fury:

> The war, which was so cruel,
> Blew off like a rainstorm,
>
> Leaving crumpled huts
> And houses with burnt thatched roofs.
>
> Today I pass this ruined and charred village
> With casual steps.
>
> The only thing that Heaven has spared
> Is an old clay pot on a storage platform,
>
> Reminding me that I, like the clay pot
> Have been spared.

The villagers who have returned
Look up from the ruins toward the distant hills.

The sky is as blue as ever.
In the autumn sun of Toriwon

A fragile cosmos
Shivers in the breeze.

The near-total destruction of Toriwon and many other villages in the area and incalculable military and civilian casualties were the price the ROK (Republic of Korea) paid for staying the Communist forces along the Naktong River and preventing them from overtaking all of South Korea. The poet, far from congratulating his luck in having survived, feels that he just happens to have been spared, "like the clay pot." The shivering fragile cosmos of the last stanza is a fitting emblem for the hapless and helpless Korean people.

Cho's "Here Lies a Communist Soldier" is a gentle and poignant expression of the sorrow of losing an "enemy." In "At Tabuwon" also Cho takes sorrowful notice of the corpses of Communist soldiers:

The corpse of a Communist soldier
Seeming to weep in remorse.

We were brothers under the same sky
Until a short while ago.

The ineffable sense of spirituality and refined perception of beauty that are the trademarks of Cho Chi-hun are not prominent features of the poems in Before the Tribunal of History, but these quiet and spare poems are beautiful and moving in a unique way.

Yu Ch'i-hwan is a poet of more passionate and overtly romantic temperament, so his poems tend to work more directly on our emotions. But in most of the war poems published in his *With the Foot Soldier*, his statements are severely disciplined and restrained. "With the Simplicity of a Child" is saved from sentimentality and made poignant by its extreme simplicity:

> With boughs and leaves sticking out of helmet and uniform
> The soldier has fallen asleep like an innocent baby,
> Curled up while waiting for a command.
>
> Hundreds of miles from home,
> The soldier expects no letters from kin.
> But he visits home in his dreams,
> So he has treasure in his heart.
>
> He can be so at peace
> Because he has set no price on his life
> And has let go of his attachment to life, like bad karma.
>
> The soldier sleeps like a flower,
> With the simplicity of a child.

Having paid tribute to the ROK soldier, Yu, in "Like a Wildflower," voices his compassion for the Communist soldier.

> Where the battle raged like a nightmare
> Last night,
> The corpse of a young enemy soldier remains
> Like a lone wildflower.
>
> Life's cruel tempest that drove you here
> Like a hunted animal
> Has dissipated,
> Leaving you this spot for your rest.
> Now your ears are opened,

Your soul is awake.
You'll hear the deep currents of the East Sea
Merging with eternity.

The unpredictability of the fortunes of war and the futility of it all
are admirably captured by Yu in a poem entitled "A Short Rest":

Soldiers are shaking off the dust of battle
By the shore of this lake in the quiet twilight.

Anxiously exhaling cigarette smoke,
Are you thinking of your family and hometown?

Friendship and hostility
Are transitory, like all human feelings.

This morning the foe fled this wind and landscape
You are unexpectedly savoring this evening.

In "The Meaning of Flags," the poet notes, not with irony but
simply as a fact of life, that although ideological strife is devouring
millions of lives and tearing the country to shreds, ideology means
nothing to simple folk:

In a lonely seaside village
On the shore of the boundless East Sea,

A flag flaps in the wind.
Yesterday it was their flag; today it is ours.

The wretched villagers, washed and bleached by waves
Through endless lonely time

Just go on,
No matter which flag flaps above them.

Few Koreans, however, were fortunate enough to be allowed to remain unconcerned about ideology. In many villages, half the population was wiped out when one side took over, and the other half when the other did, as accumulated resentments were played out in the name of lofty ideologies. Nonetheless, the fact that the number of people who fled, or tried to flee, the Communists out-numbered by many times the number of people who fled, or tried to flee, the Republic of Korea's domination can be taken as proof that Communists were more feared than South Korean "democ-rats." Many people were grateful to the ROK soldiers who fought to repel the Communists and gave their lives to guard the country. Compassion for the Communist soldiers notwithstanding, the expressions of gratitude for the ROK soldiers, their valor and their dedication, find many eloquent expressions. Anti-war sentiment was as strong as could be, but it did not cause the soldiers' valor to be discredited and maligned. On the contrary, appreciation for the soldiers' sacrifice was a core component of anti-war sentiment.

There was a perception even then that the war was a result not so much of the ideological clash between Koreans as of a power game between the superpowers, and that Koreans were helpless pawns in that game. There was, nevertheless, genuine gratitude to the American and other U.N. forces who came across half the world to "save" South Korea from Communist domination. Yu Ch'i-hwan's "To a Dead United Nations Soldier" and "To Major Den Audin" are sincere tributes to those soldiers who gave their lives to fight Communists, the enemies of freedom.

But not only soldiers suffered great physical hardships and died. Civilians suffered in other ways, but just as harshly. "Drifters" is a tribute to the tough resiliency which enabled the Korean people to survive the sub-human conditions of life in Pusan, where almost half the population of South Korea had taken refuge:

Look at the crowd of people

Thronging like a tangled heap of rubbish
On this street brushed by the cold waves of winter solstice.
The men have left behind pride and shame and attachment
And are offering for sale anything that will fetch a few pennies:
Their cherished furniture, clothes, shoes,
Even their wives' underwear.

In "Port of Glory," Yu commemorates the energy generated by the refugees packing Pusan, living in the most miserable and squalid of conditions but united by the will to survive. "My Fatherland" is a fine statement of love for one's fatherland, not only in spite of its defects but because of them. Perhaps only the people of a country that has suffered one misfortune after another, as well as repeated threats to its very continuance, can understand that love. Yu Ch'i-hwan was motivated to declare his love for his woebegone fatherland by reading an article on Korea written by a foreign correspondent:

You wrote that there's no other country in the world
Whose land is so covered with festering sores,
Where the stench of excrement assails you everywhere you go,
Where every creature to ever plague mankind thrives—
Flea, bedbug, mosquito, centipede, venomous snake, leech—
Whose people are
Pickpockets, swindlers, beggars, corrupt officials or scoundrels.
You say this country's worse than New Guinea,
That it's a country you'd like to hand over to the enemy as punishment.
Then you ask, "What crimes have we committed that we have to fight
        for a country like this?"

I am a beggar child of that country.
I stay by its side
And weep over it all the time.

("My Fatherland")

In "At the Armistice Line," Yu protests to God, who shows little concern for a hapless nation continuing to exist in hell for so long:

> God!
> How can we call Your attention to our plight?...
>
> This moment calls for Your intervention,
> And cannot end without Your final judgment.
> Are You holding back because it's still too early for You to step in?
> Are You standing by letting humans commit these iniquities
> So their final repentance will be stark?
>
> God!
> Do You remain aloof to make us grovel and supplicate?
> God, why are You swaying nonchalantly on a blade of grass shaking in
>   the breeze of noon?
> God, how can You rest easily each night in Ursa Major?

This poem voices the sense of utter loss many Koreans felt at the time about "Heaven's intention." Throughout history, the majority of Koreans, who were helpless as babes before the despotism of those in power, clung to the belief that "Heaven is not unfeeling," that, even though great injustices are the lot of many, they do not escape the notice of Heaven, which will redress them in the course of time. That the Heaven they had always relied on permitted atrocious carnage and heartbreak on such a massive scale and did nothing to put a stop to it was a blow to the very root of Koreans' belief in the existence of Divine, or Universal, Justice.

Ku Sang is a poet of compassion. He has enjoyed popularity for many decades because his poetry is accessible to most readers. He looks at what happens to ordinary people with compassion tinged with a bit of irony—just the right combination for most Korean readers. His poetry, though not difficult and complicated, has depth and insight that satisfies the serious reader. His *Poetry on Burnt Ground* sequence, which was written from the rear lines during the war, is a meditation on the sad and absurd state of his war-devastated country. On his "burnt ground," which is what Korea was during and after the war, young women have to sell their flesh to stay alive, and children mock and persecute such young women (sarcastically dubbed "western princesses"), yet with their next breath, try to lure American soldiers to patronize those very women.

In the famous second section of the sequence, the poet happens to be sitting opposite a tired woman, who out of desperate necessity had prostituted herself, and her mixed-blood boy in a night train. The boy frets, and the mother tries to pacify him. The poet offers the boy caramels out of his pocket, and the boy climbs into the poet's lap. The boy's mother, exhausted from her battle with life and her taxing role as mother of a mixed-blood child, falls asleep. The boy, also, falls asleep in the poet's lap, so that to all appearances the poet has become the father of the mixed-blood boy. To fully appreciate the poet's predicament, it must be seen in the light of the extreme prejudice Koreans have against mixed-blood children. To look as if he had fathered a child with a black woman is an indignity a man of his class and temperament could hardly bear. But the poet, imagining the few dollars that must have brought the boy into being, shudders at the cheap price of human life, hugging the innocent child breathing peacefully in his lap. He sees the face of all Koreans on the tired and abandoned face of the woman, who has to raise the mixed-blood child amid prejudice and discrimination, even outright persecution, in expiation of the sin of selling herself, a sin in which all Koreans are implicated. The poet is thus suggesting that all Korean men recognize their paternal obligation to mixed-blood children.

Beyond having to cope with the aftermath of the war, the poet also sees the need to heal the rupture of the country. In section seven, subtitled "At the cemetery of enemy soldiers," Ku, a devout Catholic, muses:

> We were bound to you in life
> By ties of hate.
> But now, your lingering resentments
> Are my responsibility
> And are incorporated in my prayers.

In section nine, subtitled "At the time of the armistice negotiations," he likens his fatherland to Sim Ch'ŏng, the legendary filial daughter who sold herself to sailors as a human sacrifice to be offered to appease the wrath of the sea god: a helpless victim at the mercy of the superpowers. Min Jae-shik in his poem "Scapegoats" likened Korea to "a chip in the superpowers' poker game." This perception of the utter inability of Korea to determine its own fate evoked both self-pity and self-derision in many poets and intellectuals, who shared a violent hatred of those corrupt politicians and entrepreneurs who exploited the country and compounded its maladies. But Ku Sang concludes the sequence by exhorting his compatriots to sow seeds of life on the ruin that is his fatherland, "So that they will bloom on our graves/ And testify to our resurrection."

Yu Ch'un-do, the only poet in this collection to have been a Communist sympathizer and to have worked for and with them, has different identifications for friend and enemy, but the war reflected in her eyes is just as absolute an evil. This successful medical doctor, who turned to poetry in her seventies, was a fifth-year medical student when the Korean War broke out. She was forced to work as a doctor in the absence of enough trained medical personnel, first for the South Korean wounded and then for the North Korean soldiers when most of the country was taken over by the Communists. In "Destiny," Yu records the beginning of her affiliation with Communists, in which she had no choice, with fine irony: the setting and the figures are the same as they were the day before with South Korean soldiers. There are only minute differences: the insignia on the soldiers' caps and a stronger odor of sweat. But those things made for heartache, imprisonment, torture and bitterness for many decades:

> I go to the outpatients' clinic with my assignment slip.
> Yesterday's wounded ROK soldiers are nowhere in sight,
> And only a doctor and a nurse pace the empty room.
> Jeeps carrying wounded soldiers arrive
> In the hospital yard.
>
> Some are carried in on stretchers, some hobble in leaning on others,
> And some hop in on one leg.
> Beyond the window, the sight is the same as yesterday's,
> Except they have red stars on their caps and a stronger odor of sweat.
> The doctor and the nurse do the same things they did yesterday.
> Is that the spirit of the Red Cross?
>
> Our destiny of parting, death, and imprisonment
> Began that day.
> The bitterness of many decades lay in wait.

While sharing the pains and agonies of the wounded North Koreans in a field hospital with insufficient equipment and medical supplies, she came to feel a close human bond with them and a deep respect for their ideology. Then, when the North Koreans were pushed back, she tried to follow them north but was prevented by the American bombing, as described in "The Girl Soldier and the Moon." Afterward, while trying to find her way to her hometown, she was captured by a South Korean soldier. Rescued from summary execution by the ROK soldier, thanks to the timely intervention of a passing American officer (described in

"Kŭmgang River Ghost"), she was sent to prison as a prisoner of war, walking in a long and terrifying march delineated in "Let's Take Our Own Lives." In the prison for Communists she witnesses horrors that remain indelible, as sketched in "In Ch'ŏngju Prison." Released from the prison with the help of an acquaintance, she was able to join her family in her hometown but was subjected to several imprisonments and torture as a "collaborator," as told in "Crickets Chirping in My Ear." After the war, Yu was able to hide that portion of her life and go on to become a successful gynecologist and wife of an eminent scholar—an enviable woman to all outward appearance. But she says that a half-century later she still suffers nightmares and wakes up crying. After her husband died and she retired from active practice, she decided to bear witness to her nation's history as she saw and experienced it, hoping to gain relief from her tormenting memories by making them public. Although her prosody lacks sophistication, her guileless verses effectively convey the most dramatic and terrifying experiences a human being can live through.

Yu Ch'un-do's poems remind us that war was not easier on women. Admittedly, she was a special case, and she was in a sense an active participant rather than a passive sufferer. For the majority of women who could do nothing but suffer, the agonies, anxiety, and heartbreak of war were excruciating. But very few poems by women delineating the life of women behind the front lines remain. Some of Mo Yun-suk's poems express the agonies of newlywed brides waiting for husbands who went to war and were not heard from again and other predicaments of women, but they lack a sense of immediacy as the poet herself led a far different life. In the poem translated in this collection, "What the Dead Soldier Said," she writes as an "official" poet of South Korea. Through the persona of a newly-dead soldier of the Republic of Korea, she makes ringing assertions about guarding the country not just until the end of his life but until the end of Time:

> I gladly forego a grave for my body
> Or even a small coffin to shield me from wind and rain.
> Soon rough winds will whip my body
> And worms will feast on my flesh,
> But I will gladly be their companion.
> My ardent wish is to become a handful of earth
> In this valley in my fatherland
> Waiting for better times
> For my brethren.

Poetry written by men who actually participated in war expresses as resolute a determination to fight but is less rhetorical and more anchored to concrete battle situations. In Pak Il-song's "The Eyes of the Sentry," the sentry's eyes are so piercing that "Not even an ant/ Would risk trying/ Your vigilance." Chang Ho-gang, a career soldier who attained the rank of a general before retirement, dug numerous trenches to repel the enemy:

> We dig, build, install, and bury
> Firing trenches, shelter trenches, wire fences, and mines
> In a tight network
> So that even a swarm of enemies skilled in night maneuvers
> Couldn't penetrate our defense,
> Even by burrowing underground like moles.
>
> ("Kansas Line")

Chang's desire for the country's unification is so intense that he wants his body to lie exposed to the weather if he falls in battle so his bones will crumble to dust, be blown by the wind, and dropped in Ch'ŏnji Lake, the crater lake on top of Mt. Paekdu on the northern border of Korea.

Yi Yun-su, in "The Foot Soldier Marches," declares his resolution to march to the end of the earth and till the end of his life in defense of the country:

> We march everywhere,
> We march in silence.
> We march, bathed in sweat,
> Our bodies sizzling in the sun.
> We march along endless dusty country roads.
> We wade through rivers if bridges are destroyed.
> We push through like tanks on roads tanks can't run.
> We march with iron will and high spirit.
> We march through rain, clasping guns whose straps dig into our
>   shoulders.
> We march through mud,
> We march over felled trees,
> And navigate through forests...
>
> We march until the soles of our boots feel like red-hot iron.
> We can go everywhere, we go everywhere.
> When we can't walk, we crawl.
> Nothing can stop us now.

Many of the poems express hatred of the enemy and the determination to exterminate them, but in an impersonal way. Often, expressions of hatred and contempt for the enemy are tinged with regret, as in Mun Sang-myŏng's "The Blackout Line":

> The real enemies
> Are those whose souls
> Live in darkness.
> They think and act without light.
> If only they had the conscience
> To love light,
> I would be driving a golden carriage

Brimming with happy songs
Over this hill clad in autumn foliage,
Speeding toward the Diamond Mountains
Scattering laughter in the wind.

It is remarkable that even the combatants, whose lives were constantly endangered by the enemy and who witnessed so many of their comrades killed and wounded, regarded the enemy with sorrow and compassion once the enemy was dead or captured. This is due to the peculiar paradox and tragedy of the Korean War noted earlier: Koreans regard the whole nation as "blood kin descended from the same original forefather, Tangun," and the enemy could turn out to be a neighbor or a brother. Yu Ch'un-do, contemplating the young North Korean soldier whose his leg was amputated without anaesthesia, shudders at the thought that her brother, who was about the same age as the boy, "might be aiming his gun at us as a soldier of the Republic" ("The Emergency Field Hospital"). And Yu Chŏng has a hallucinatory sense that "Those emaciated shoulders heaving in pitch darkness/ I glimpsed while peering across the frozen 38th Parallel" are without a doubt those of his brother, who had run away from home with the family bull ("Brothers").

The thought of brother killing brother is something too horrible to contemplate to a Korean, for whom family ties traditionally took precedence over the needs and rights of the individual. Therefore, many imagined reconciliations have been suggested. Kim Kyu-dong's "A Grave" is a rhapsody on the imagined brotherhood of a North Korean and a south Korean soldier achieved after death through being buried in one grave. Pak Pong-u, in "Blooming on the Wasteland" also dreams of the day when North and South Koreans can cross the border as freely as butterflies.

The soldier-poets exhibit staunch determination and courage, but nowhere in their poetry is war glorified. War itself, more than the enemy, is condemned for causing all the tragedy and suffering. In "The Ridge of Blood," Yi Tŏk-chin shuddered at the carnage of a war that not only altered the landscape but seemed to make the earth a gigantic maw of death:

> Flesh bursts and blood spurts,
> And streams of crimson dye the surrounding valleys red.
> The landscape changes as corpses pile up,
> And the ridge becomes a bloodthirsty devil.

Mun Sang-myŏng also mourned the innumerable lives given without any discernible effect:

> Over four-hundred-thousand shells and bullets were fired
> On this hill where the death agonies of innumerable soldiers
> Consumed the mystery of eons
> And lives fell like grass and twigs.
> Ah, the blood that ran down the hill
> In a flood!
>
> ("White Horse Hill")

At the National Cemetery, the same poet muses on the futility of lives sacrificed in war:

> In the space where thought is aflame
> The sun has lost heat,
> Driving the pigeons home.
> But these silent witnesses
> To wounds
> Nothing can heal
> Keep their silence
> Till the end of time.
>
> ("Lost Time and Effaced Language")

In Korea, it is never counted a weakness in brave soldiers to harbor nostalgia. Nor have I encountered in the literature of any country any blame that redounded on a soldier for yearning for his home, family and sweetheart. Chang Ho-gang, in spite of his stout soldier's heart, cannot help yearning for home:

> Another meteor glides in silence.
> When the chirping of insects evoke memories of home,
> The soldier recalls the face of his beloved.
> The Dipper, which had been in the bead of his northward-aiming rifle,
> Has disappeared.
>
> ("The Armistice Line at Night")

> Tonight, after pillars of napalm fire have subsided
> And the moon and stars are weeping,
> The soldier's heart flies to his hometown in the North
> Which abounds in legends.
> Ah, who drew this Kansas Line
> That keeps the strong spirits of soldiers
> From ranging freely?
>
> ("Kansas Line")

Chang Su-ch'ŏl, "aiming straight at the enemy" while standing in a dark trench feeling his very marrow freeze, cannot help thinking of home. Unlike in times of peace, love for one's home often comes into conflict with patriotism in times of war: one can't serve both at the same time. Yi Hyo-sang notes this conflict in "Fatherland" as an astonishing and painful discovery. First, the sense of a long-suffering fatherland in imminent danger inspires boundless loyalty and love:

> I never loved my fatherland as dearly as now.
> I didn't know one's fatherland was such a precious thing.
> I realize for the first time that my life is a mere feather weighed against
>   my fatherland.
> I realize belatedly that your fatherland is something

You embrace with death looking over your shoulder.

But giving up a son in defense of a country one loves even so dearly is far from easy, as Yi realizes in "War":

> The day I sent my servants, nephews, cousins on Mother's side,
> Cousins on Father's side, and a hundred youths from the village to the
> > war,
> I made a moving speech, with words welling up from my heart.
> But the day I sent my son, the thought that I was a hypocrite
> Smote my conscience.
>
> The day I sent my beloved son to the war
> I wished I could fight in his place.

Fighting a war for a country like Korea required true loyalty and spirit of sacrifice, since the country was so weakened that it could not compensate its citizens for their sacrifices and losses in its defense:

> Your meritorious service in the war
> Should bring you glory and rewards.
>
> But our hungry and threadbare country
> Can give you nothing.
>
> Even if you leave the perilous armed forces
> A troubled society awaits you.
>
> Destroyed cities and ruined villages
> Stand on denuded hills and valleys gone dry.
> > (Chang Ho-gang, "Dedicating a Flower")

At the time of the Korean War, the country was so torn apart and people were so battered by emotional, physical and material suffering that there was little hope for comfort, to say nothing of prosperity, and despair was all too pervasive. Hope for a better future was something as fragile as a common flower, but also as definite as the will of the plant to bloom:

At whose request have you bloomed on this wasteland where men slaughtered men, you nameless flower that confronts the sky with your fragile sweetness? How can you, a delicate plant standing upon your frail stalk on a sunny road beneath blue heaven, efface, with your ineffable smile, the deafening din of cannons and bombs, and the screams and bloodbaths that shook the earth to its core?

(Pak Yang-kyun, "Flower")

Korea's survival owes entirely to people having held on to that fragile hope.

Translator's Acknowledgments

I would like to express my gratitude to my collaborator, Professor James A. Perkins of Westminster College for his valuable advice and emendations. Dr. Perkins, a poet in his own right, was in Korea as a Fulbright exchange professor in the fall semester of 1998. I am also indebted to Professor Jong-gil Kim, my former colleague at the Korea University and a renowned poet, for bringing many of the poems in this collection to my notice and also for going over my translations of Yu Ch'i-hwan's poems and suggesting alternatives. I am also grateful to many other friends who helped with the excavation of some forgotten poems, most notably Professor Lee Ki-yun of Korea Military Academy. Professor Ohn Chang-il of KMA helped me with the names of weaponry. My appreciation also goes to to retired General Chang Ho-gang, Mr. Kim Kwang-rim, and Mr. Min Chae-shik for their permission to include their poems in this collection.

Thanks are also due to Dennis Maloney and Elaine LaMattina of White Pine Press for their excellent editorial advice and work on production of this book.

—Suh Ji-moon
Seoul, April 2002

Before the Tribunal of History
Poems by Cho Chi-hun
■

Journal of Despair (June 25, 1950)

I was sleeping like a log
In my hut on Sŏngbuk-dong hill
With the doors open.
Awakened suddenly,
I see Mogwol standing outside.

"How can you sleep?
Special editions are flying in the streets," Mogwol scolds.
"The communists are invading."

I light a cigarette, pretending calm.
I knew this was bound to happen.
And it has come at last.

A chill fills my heart.
My thoughts, which were drifting lightly as a cloud, are stilled.
Something resembling sorrow flits over my heart.

I feel no tremor.

Journal of Despair (June 26, 1950)

Two o'clock in the afternoon,
I'm lecturing on poetics in a third-floor classroom of Korea University.

I hear the noise of guns from the direction of Ŭijŏngbu.
The loudspeaker on the campus tremulously relays news from the
    battlefront.

Youths seem to regard poetry as irrelevant to the moment.
But it is at moments of crises that poetry can be our support.

"Now you'll realize the meaning of the anxiety of being,"
I tell them.

Saddened by the possibility that after parting today
They may not meet again,
Students close their eyes to still the tumult in their hearts.

How precious and noble is the affection
That makes them mourn parting from friends
At this desperate juncture.

Pushing the door open and coming out into the hallway,
I see poetry sucked away by the smoke of battle.

The hill is draped with dense cannon smoke.
At sunset Mognam came for a visit.

Seoul will have to be abandoned, he said.
So, what are we going to do?

Well, what can we do?
My heart feels like lead.
Mognam says he knows the feeling,

And that's why he sought me out.

Who can remain calm
In the face of the terror of death?

"Let us not seek to prolong life
At the cost of our honor."

The willpower fired by that resolution
Enables me to face death today.

Be grateful
For this short hour of reprieve.

Journal of Despair (June 27, 1950)

Members of my family bid each other good-bye.
We will meet again if we're lucky.

The joy of the little one in his new garb
Sears my heart for a long time.

Father said,
"Don't take life too lightly; avoid courting death."

I go to see Tongni.
Mognam had said he'd be there, too.

The landlord comes back with borrowed rice.
We share rice gruel with his family.

Midang stands before the microphone
At the emergency national radio station.

"Dear fellow citizens,
What should be our resolve during this crisis?"

Words so commonplace,
But tears flow from my eyes.

Who among those fleeing with sacks and bundles
Would pay any heed to his message?

A poet's words
Rouse only the poet himself.

We decide to hold a sit-in protest
In the basement of the artists' union.

Once you have hardened your will, death is but fulfillment.
But I hate a lonely death.

At the Defense Ministry's office we drink
To the recapture of Ŭijŏngbu.

Colonel Kim Hyŏn-su
In blue combat gear!

I say I'll drink all the liquor and die drunk,
But my dear friends urge me to leave.

"The only duty left us is to blow up this radio station
After asking the people's forgiveness and appealing to the world
            to save us,"

Says Colonel Kim, hugging me.
How true!

I know that a truthful person
Tells the truth even when he can't act on his words.

Of the many who promised to join the sit-in
Not even one has shown up. It's eleven o'clock.

Only four of us, dead drunk, came out to the drizzling night street.
Midang, Mogwol, Mognam, and I.

We go to a friend's in Wonhyoro
And fall asleep listening to the final broadcast.

"My country, my compatriots, my land!"
The announcer's resonant voice is hoarse.

People have left, but voices remain.
Voices are enough to assure us, bear us company.

Thunder roars, like the whip of an angry God.
What need for this reprimand?
Our escape is already cut off.

This shore of the Han River is the last stronghold of Seoul.
We plug our ears and try to fall asleep.
I hear stifled sobbing.

Journal of Despair (June 28, 1950)

Where can we go, with the river in our face and the enemy
          pressing us from behind?
I feel sweat breaking out on my forehead.

At breakfast the rice tastes like sand.
I wet my throat with the broth,
But rice refuses to go down my throat.

Does our consciousness govern our body
So absolutely?

Hundreds of thousands have poured out
To Mapo, the exploded footbridge, Sŏbinggo and Kwangnaru.

Red flags, red songs, and red tanks hem us in
From all sides,

And I have no cigarettes to give me even momentary relief.
There are only five rowboats on the river.

Ah, my family and friends must be in this crowd.
But where can we go, hedged in between the enemy
          and the river?

At last, from a hidden cliff
A man jumps down toward a rowboat.

A desperate jump!
Probably, like most of us, he doesn't know how to swim.

The sky, so bright and clear after rain, looks cruel,
Lighting up the shore of despair.

Death is deferred for a moment.

A Pledge

How can I temper this fervid heart
Even hugging an icy eons-old rock cannot cool?

I'll bite my lips in the darkness
And smear my blood on pale flowers

To inject my life into them
And die with the morning sun.

I weep at your touch,
My beloved, radiant as the holy sun and moon.

I'll weep until nothing remains but my bleached bones,
Until I'm resurrected and die again,

Although bereft of all I love.
I'm poor at heart

And have no presents or medals to offer my beloved.
I have only a flute cut from a bamboo stalk
That grew on a spot watered by the blood of righteous men.

Beloved, do you hear the flute's weeping strain
Ringing to the Heavens?

How can I help yearning for you, beloved?
I shall weep, calling your name,

Until the day all hatred melts away
And my red heart becomes charcoal,
And the charcoal burns to cinder again.

Return Victorious

to soldiers at the front

With only two finger-thin pickles as garnish,
Or only a few scoops of red pepper paste,
You swallow the barley-and-rice meal hungrily.
How long has it been since you've eaten?
You said that your gun kept slipping from your grasp
While you fought in the pouring rain
After a three-day fast.
You pinch yourself to stay awake and bite your lips to suppress
       hunger,
But the humble M1s are not fit instruments
To vent your fury toward the assaulting tanks.
Your eyes are swollen
From shedding torrents of angry tears.

My beloved younger brothers!

Know that yours and yours alone will be the power and the glory
Of saving the country and guarding freedom.
What makes you push on and on
With hungry stomachs and exhausted bodies?
You say you need your salary
Only to replace your tattered boots.
Asking no other recompense from anyone
You dedicate your all
For the glory of our country.
You stand by your code of honor, cost what it may.
We know that the only fit reward for you
Is unification of our country and the victory of justice.
Nothing else can compensate your sacrifice.

Beloved brethren, guardians of this land!

We will be victorious.
Have injustice and evil ever gone unpunished?
The entire nation is behind you,
And the whole free world supports you.
We believe you will return
Bearing joyful news of victory
As your gift to anxious compatriots.
We live for the day.
Return victorious, soldiers of honor!
We await you with open arms,
You Heaven-sent guardian angels!

(July 10, 1950)

Written from the Combat Front

Life is not so fragile as I had thought.

Even when shot in the side or chest, unless the divine spirit is blown out of its mysterious seat in each and every cell, the soldiers keep charging at the enemy.

Ah, such tenacity of life is given only to those who are ready to give away their lives.

After the tempest of guns, the village is empty of men and animals.

Although ripe crops rot in the fields, terrified villagers stay on the windy hills, eating grass.

Their tears of righteous fury divide them from beasts, though they wander like animals.

Only those with tenacity for life
Know that death gives life value.

Romantic Army Life

from the army writers' camp

Our camp, unguarded by any sentry,
Is an old hut with a plank wall and a pomegranate tree in the yard.

We become more romantic
The more precarious life becomes.

In the sweltering heat of August
We sit bare-chested playing chess,
Drink rice wine and snack on pickled apples
Even on nights bombs explode.
But at the command of the officer
We take up our arms—pen and paper—
And prepare for combat on desk, chessboard, floor and verandah,
Vying to occupy the most strategic points.

This is our battlefield, from which we fire paper bullets to slash
        the enemy's heart.
Here we shed silent tears, longing for our families and friends,
And here we write them letters saying,
"We'll be in Seoul soon."

Soldiers without weapons,
We carry cyanide in our vests.

The pomegranate which was green when we first came
Has ripened and splits open.

Yes, in the backyard of the army writers' camp
A self-exploding pomegranate screams at the sky.

(August 30, 1950, Taegu)

At Ch'ŏngma's Temporary Residence

When T'ongyŏng fell to the communists during the war, Ch'ŏngma took up temporary residence in Pusan. Midang, who took ill while staying in besieged Taegu, went to Ch'ŏngma's abode to recuperate. Shortly before the recapture of Seoul on the 28th of September, I went there, too, and stayed with them for a few days.

Looking at the sea
Sitting on worn rattan chairs,

We feel autumn stealing up our backs
And touching us on the shoulders.

When the puppy's steps crush the dead leaves
We call out the names of dear ones.

Our lives are ephemeral as the fallen leaves,
And soon we will have to return to our source.

Have pity on us, persimmon leaves,
And take your time in turning red.

Above the roof
Airplanes fly dizzily.

(September 5, 1950)

At *Tabuwon*

Coming to Tabuwon after the month-long siege is lifted,
I see autumn clouds dappling its hills.

After the cannon roar raged for a month
Attacking and defending,

I realize how near Taegu
Tabuwon is located.

To keep this small village
As part of our free republic

Even grass and shrubbery
Had to die.

Oh, do not ask
For what Cause
The land had to suffer such ruin.

The head of a war horse
Severed while rearing toward heaven.

The corpse of a Communist soldier
Seeming to weep in remorse.

We were brothers under the same sky
Until a short while ago.

Now, though cooled by the autumn breeze,
Tabuwon stinks, like rotting fish.

If there were no Fate governing life and death
And we had no faith in Fate's purpose,

What rest could there be for these pitiful dead?

The Tabuwon I survived to see
Offers no repose to the living or the dead.
Only the wind stirs it.

(September 26, 1950)

At Toriwon

The war, which was so cruel,
Blew off like a rainstorm,

Leaving huts crumpled
And houses with burnt thatched roofs.

Today I pass this ruined and charred village,
Stepping casually.

The only thing that heaven has spared
Is an old clay pot on a storage platform,

Reminding me that I, like the clay pot,
Have been spared.

The villagers who have returned
Look up from the ruins toward the distant hills.

The sky is as blue as ever.
In the autumn sun of Toriwon

A fragile cosmos
Shivers in the breeze.

(September 26, 1950)

Here Lies a Communist Soldier

In the midst of hot pursuit
Through Ŭisŏng, Andong, and the Chukryŏng Pass,

I jump down from the truck to slake my thirst
And touch the roadside daisies.

A chalk inscription on a piece of wood
Stuck in the grass catches my eye.

"Here lies a Communist soldier."

The boy lying beside it
Still breathes faintly.

His limbs, covered with dark blood, are rotting,
And his half-opened eyes cannot see.

You must have crept to this stream
And quaffed long drafts to allay your thirst and pain.

This is your country, too.
Did you smell the earth of your hometown here?

Whether enemy or brother,
You are a human being,
A sacred creature deserving love.

Who dares add further injury
To this bruised soul?

His dying face shows
His sorrow at leaving those he loves.
Death offers no transcendence.

A piece of wood
Inscribed with a tender and sad heart

Tells of cruel battle
Under the clear blue autumn sky:

"Here lies a Communist soldier."

(September 26, 1950)

The Battle of Chukryŏng Pass

An old prophet said, "This is a land the fire of battle cannot enter." The prophecy must have lost power. It was also predicted that P'unggi would be a land of eternal victory. But the sun sets over the market site of P'unggi, turned to a heap of ashes. On the steep Chukryŏng Pass, which winds like sheep's intestines, we pursue the fleeing enemy.

The leaves have prematurely turned red, spattered with human blood. Even the moss on rocks has turned blood red. A tank sits melted in a shower of fire. A burnt corpse has shriveled to the size of a puppy. His spilled brain is thickly crusted with ants.

To fear death here is not so much a luxury as stupidity. Under a dark sky, cannons spit fire incessantly. Chukryŏng Pass twists like the innards of sheep. Our truck crawls along with headlights dimmed.

The brilliant stars brighten our hearts, but frightening cliffs gape beneath, and Tanyang is still far away.

(September 27, 1950)

On Returning to Seoul

I round the hill of Manguri
And enter Seoul!

I doubted I would return alive,
But Seoul greets me after ninety days of battle.

I am thankful for every face I meet.
To have lived is a gift to fellow citizens.

The welcoming waves and cheers of those who remained
Bring tears to my eyes.

My country is my conscience,
But I came back without any record of service to show.

My family has returned to our abandoned house;
They are weeding the yard.

My wife had taken refuge in a temple
Crossing a steep hill at night crying, leading the children by the
        hand.

She was out again already,
To retrieve the things she'd left with a neighbor.

I hug and kiss my three-year-old, who has oozing sores
From eating acorns.

My six-year-old says he loved the taste of crayfish
He fished from the stream and grilled over fire.

Poor things, you could have died,
Having a father powerless to protect you.

My heart ached with guilt thinking of you.
I had no other anxiety in the world.

My father must have loved me
As I do my little ones.

Father isn't back,
Though the son he worried about has come back alive.

Only his glasses and razor are back,
Retrieved from the enemy.

There is no news of my mother, gone to her hometown
Which the enemy later occupied.

Now, past thirty years of age, I realize in vain
How deep and strong one's love for his kin can be.

Without waiting to see my wife
I leave my house to return to duty.
This is wartime: how can I neglect my duty for the sake of private
        affection?

In the editorial office of the government newspaper
Sŏkch'ŏn grabs my hand and weeps.

"Yŏngnang is dead," he says,
His face a mask of sorrow.

I go to what had been Myŏngdong.
I run into a friend who survived in a hideout.

My heart is too full even to hug him.
We just gaze at each other.

Grand Forks Public Library

Boarding a truck at sunset
I go to the command post in Uidong.

I tell Mogwol to leave the post to me and go home
Since he doesn't know whether his family is alive.

Brigadier General R welcomes me with a smile.
"I didn't expect you to show up tonight,
This night of your family's reunion."

I return home walking the dark road
Unarmed, murmuring the password.

The war orphan I picked up in Tonamli
Seems to have forgotten his name and his age.

(October 3, 1950)

At a Tavern in Pongilch'ŏn

I leave for Pyongyang, in search of my beloved. To hear news of my beloved if not to see her.

No one offers me a seat on an airplane, nor even in a military truck. My name is not on the list of writers and artists to be dispatched to Pyongyang.

I will go to Pyongyang even if I have to walk every step of the way. Unsam and Chaech'un volunteered to accompany me. Crossing the Nokbŏnli Pass, we rest at a tavern in Pongilch'ŏn in P'aju.

On a passing truck young men and women are singing military marches and middle-aged women are shouting in heavy accents. Happy faces returning home. No one stops his car for me.

Had I better sleep in P'aju tonight? The sun is sinking over the tavern in Pongilch'ŏn and I have to walk all the way to Pyongyang.

(October, 1950)

You Are Crossing the Thirty-Eighth Parallel

Crouching in a corner of a military truck,
I fall asleep while looking at myriad stars.

If we put up at Haeju tonight,
We'll reach Pyongyang at nightfall tomorrow.

A sudden merciless bullet
Rips the earth.

As we round a bend of a hill
It starts to rain.

The shot was to warn people of Communist stragglers.
We have only one M1 rifle on the truck.

The young lieutenant is happy,
Heading for home.

Headlights suddenly illuminate a sign.
"You are crossing the thirty-eighth parallel."

Rain falls on the thirty-eighth parallel
On either side of which stand lovers, weeping.

I cross the thirty-eighth parallel,
Heading toward a barrier of mind that seems
        to be receding all the time.

(October, 1950)

A Farmer's Hut in Yonbaek

The truck stops in the yard of a thatch-roofed hut, after driving through millet and cabbage fields and rounding a hedge.

The young lieutenant jumps down and calls "Mother!" The whole family pours out of the hut. They hug and cry and jump for joy.

The lieutenant had run away from home four years ago. Though he returned in a dirty combat uniform, he is given a hero's welcome.

A sleepy chicken is killed and cooked, noodles are pressed, and the feast begins. Though a stranger, I am welcomed like an old friend. Happiness bubbles over into smiles and laughter.

The moon comes out of the clouds. We board the truck again at midnight. The mother frets about her son not being able to spend one night at home.

That's how Korean mothers grow old, their eyelashes hardly ever dry. I see my mother in her. My mother—in everybody's hometown!

(October, 1950)

Heartless Taedong River

The streets of Pyongyang are deserted.

On the shore of the Taedong River a captured female Communist guerrilla in rough hemp blouse and skirt is being led away, a Soviet-made carbine slung from her shoulder.

A lonely stranger with nowhere to go, I sit on a bench under the trees lining Stalin Street.

Ten years ago, I walked all the way from Wonsan to Pyongyang, past Yangdŏk and Sunch'ŏn. They were laying the P'yŏng-won railway then.

I had only twelve pennies in my pocket, so I turned back with a desolate smile, unable to buy even a dish of cold noodles.

I vowed never to visit Pyongyang again without a full pocket, but here I am. Why?

I climb the Taedong Gate terrace and gaze at the flowing water. It is ten years since I muttered "Heartless Taedong River!" Ah, flowing rivers are always heartless. Was the Han like this on the day Seoul fell?

(October, 1950)

Poetry on the Wall

God, make my heart beat faster.
Time, make my arms stronger.
We were given new lives on this land in your name.
And it must be your will that fiends are ravaging it.

Warmer days used to succeed cold days in Korean winters
But this year a northwest wind keeps freezing everything.
What's the meaning of this *nalnari* tune, and what's this rusty
    sword for?

Brethren, let us have more charity toward one another.
Friends, let us hug each other with big smiles.

It will be winter solstice the day after tomorrow.
Then, long, dark nights will grow shorter.
Why should we cry in the spring, when life will be renewed?
No one can stop the seasons changing.
Behold, the throbbing of democracy impatient for the demise of
    communism!

(December 28, 1950)

At Chongro

on leaving Seoul for the second time

People left,
Locking their gates fast.

Mourning that their young nation is endangered
And tribulations beset their countrymen.

Carrying their faith in a bundle,
They disappeared to faraway corners of this land.

Evening glow from the west spreads over cold Chongro Street.
The bell remains, though the pavilion was burned down.

I hurl myself at the bell to make it ring
But the bell remains mute and my heart aches, bursting with fury.

The sound of distant cannon from all around
Highlights the silence of this street.

Unable to vent my sorrow with a full-throated cry,
My lips pucker up, despite the temperature of seventeen below.

Hating to even breathe under injustice,
Preferring to give up everything and go empty-handed,

People have fled the city once more.
Ah, the silence of Chongro, with all shop doors shuttered fast!

Now, when I, too, leave,
Communists' songs will ring through this street.

But in flowering spring
This will be our capital again.

I bury my poor song in this dark earth
Before leaving Seoul for the second time.

(January 3, 1951)

With the Foot Soldier
Poems by Yu Ch'i-hwan

■

With the Simplicity of a Child

at Yangyang

With boughs and leaves sticking out of helmet and uniform
The soldier has fallen asleep like an innocent baby,
Curled up waiting for a command.

Hundreds of miles from home
The soldier expects no letters from kin,
But he visits home in his dreams,
So he has treasure in his heart.

He can be so at peace
Because he has set no price on his life
And has released that attachment, like bad karma.

The soldier sleeps like a flower,
With the simplicity of a child.

Like a Wildflower

at Changjŏn

Where the battle raged like a nightmare
Last night,
The corpse of a young enemy soldier remains
Like a lone wildflower.

Life's cruel tempest that drove you here
Like a hunted animal
Has dissipated,
Leaving you this spot for your rest.

Now your ears are opened,
Your soul is awake.
You'll hear the deep currents of the East Sea
Merging with eternity.

At the Frontline

Where have all the villagers gone?
Not even an ant dares crawl out
Under the emptiness of noon on the frontline
Where neither we nor the enemy dare advance one step
And the cruel cannons concealed on the peaks all around
Hold the silence of death in their barrels.
The sparkling sun highlights the hollowness, like a cinematic
       freeze frame,
And broken furniture lies scattered
On the floor of the empty room
Seen over the wall felled by a bomb.
Coxcombs in the yard bloom redder than blood
In the ominous stillness of the front
Aligned for an earth-rending battle.

Beautiful Soldiers

at Chasan

After scattering the enemy,
Soldiers pour into a village.
The dark streets
Quake at the rumble of trucks and arms.
Behold!
Soldiers sitting by bonfires.
Their military garb is ragged,
Their features gaunt with battle fatigue,
But even their enemy would admire their valor.
You soldiers, the living spirit of my country,
May men of your mettle guard every inch of our homeland!

A Short Rest

at Small Lake Tungting

Beside a lake in the quietly falling dusk,
Battle-worn soldiers are resting.

Savoring your precious cigarette,
Are you thinking of your folks at home?

Friendship and hostility
Are transitory, like all human affairs.

This morning the foe fled the wind and landscape
You are quietly relishing this evening.

To My Daughter Yŏng-a

at Munch'ŏn

I lie on the sand in this pine grove
On the shore of the East Sea.

The distant cannon
Grumbles incessantly, like mankind moaning.

My little darling!
I never imagined my love for you
Would wrench my heart so.

Innumerable young men
Gave up their lives
Yesterday and today.
Here, where life is spent more cheaply
Than pennies for groceries,
Soldiers give up their only life
Without knowing whence it came or whither it goes.

My little darling,
Even though the kiss I planted on your tender cheek
May have been my last,
Put aside your love and pity for me
Like rags not worth bequeathing to anyone.

May you grow and live like a tree
My little darling,
Even in this world barren of affection.

Diamond Mountain

at Onjŏng-ri

At Onjŏngri Station at the foot of Diamond Mountain
Some of the early arrivals have fallen asleep
In the empty station filled with pure silence
After the train whistle ceased and the enemy fled.
Standing in the autumn sun of the cosmos-filled station yard,
I gaze at the gorgeous Diamond Mountain,
And the hellish war seems utterly senseless.
Eight howitzers are showering rounds
At the fleeing enemy nine thousand yards away.
Explosions tear the earth, profaning the divine peaks
And the heavens far above.
But the mountain still stands,
White clouds, like a scarf of karma, curled round its top.

The Search Squadron

at Hwajin

I haven't seen any of you
Yet,

Only the marks you left,
"Search Squadron, Unit X,"
Written with chalk
At conspicuous points along the path.

Because you open the way for us,
Taking the point
Boldly, nimbly and quietly
Braving death,

We know no retreat.
Though we can't see you, you lead us forward.

The Meaning of Flags

at Mangyang

In a lonely seaside village
On the shore of the boundless East Sea,

A flag flaps in the wind.
Yesterday it was their flag; today it is ours.

The wretched villagers, washed and bleached by waves
Through endless lonely time,

Just go on,
No matter which flag flaps above them.

Forward March

at P'och'ŏn

We stole into the village last night.
Today we have to steal away.

At three A.M.
Even before the cocks crow,

Under cold spikes of a silver-hook moon
We don combat gear, take up guns and ammo.

To show the enemy
Our iron resolve

We must bear hardship
Stoutly.

We press the trail of the enemy
Guided by the North Star.

Cowardice

at Ssangŭm

Behold the soldiers
Taking life and death in stride
Here in this field
Where an indiscriminate shower of bullets
May suddenly fly.

It is not that they hold their lives
Cheap, like pebbles on the ground;
Only one life is given to each,
And that one life is their whole world,
And their loved ones hold them dearer than heaven.

But look,
How these dauntless spirits
Disregard danger,
Treating it as but a gust of wind.

You, who cling pitifully to life,
Not knowing when to offer it worthily:
Even if you wrote a thousand books,
I would still
Hold you in contempt.

To Comrades

at Kojŏ

Two corpses just arrived on stretchers
At the regiment's medical tent
From the battlefield just eight kilometers away.

Friends-in-arms,
Two privates from some rustic village in the South.
You fought in the bloody battle of the Hyŏngsan River;

You marched day and night on bare feet, slept along the road,
And fought desperate battles, eating one portion of rice a day.
You stood penitent under your commander's harsh reprimand.
You bore cruel hardship to the thirty-eighth parallel and beyond
And gave your lives here today.

I know what hope and anguish burned
Behind your plain features and frank eyes.
I only fear there may come those
Who would glibly exploit the sacrifice you made,

Causing you to regret
The suffering and death you offered so nobly.
In the hometown for which you so keenly longed
No one knows of your brave death,
And your aged parents would weep thinking of you
If they had so much as a bowl of new rice
In the chill of morning and evening.

Beloved brothers, dear comrades! Rest in peace.
Your death will not be in vain;
You will be mourned by people
Who have to live with their grief.

Life and Death

Extinguished lamps swept aside!
You sprang out a few minutes ago
Like spirited deer.

Are you pretending to sleep, to fool us?

Or was life such a silly joke
That you ceased to bother with it
And returned to your true self?

Lieutenant Paek, head tilted a little to the left,
Sargeant Wu, one leg slung over Major Paek's chest,
Both with faces covered with white cloth,

What was so bitter
Has lost its sting.
You are beyond all that now.

Like a Red Peony

at Yŏngdŏk

Even in this tiny rustic hamlet
Armies swept in and were beaten out.
Conflict carried to extremes
Trampled and uprooted life's flowerbed.

On the lonely roads at quiet dusk
Soldiers scuttle around like honking geese.
Night's primitive desperation
Has once again overtaken men's reason.
Ah, how can we preserve our sanity
In the stark exigency of life?

A country woman brought to the sagging medical tent
With her shoulders smashed
Bleeds—a peony
Opening in the twilight!

I Ask You

at Kaljae

Thirty *li* to climb up and thirty *li* to climb down.
This steep pass at Kaljae winds like sheep's guts.
The vast ocean swells and rolls to the east,
And the Taebaek range winds endlessly to the west.
In the bright silence in between
Soldiers march, raising yellow dust,
Their heads bleached white by the sun.
At every bend and corner
Trenches dug for men to spring at men
Lurk like reptiles.
You mountains and ocean,
Tell me, if you can,
What's the point?

Fleeing the War

at Yŏnghae

Carrying tattered bundles,
People are retirning to their homes
Like swallows in the spring.
But here at this solitary house by the road
In an empty yard unguarded by even a twig gate
Only morning glories bloom and gourd vines curl.
Did people take refuge
Too far away to return?

Resolution

at Wonsan

Is human hatred such a cruel thing?
All that remains here
Is a miserable denial of human dignity.
Only wreckage remains
Of what men worked so hard to create and possess.
I cannot think of a word of consolation
For an old man squatting on the ruins of his home.
At the tip of Yŏnghŭng Bay,
The high, leaden waves of the East Sea rage,
And far down at the edge of Myŏngsashimni Beach
A group of airplanes exhibits merciless determination.
Everything in sight
Exudes intense hatred.
Ah, if this is mankind's inevitable way,
How can I avoid marching on in lonely fury?

To the East Sea

while driving on the East Coast

I finally realize, driving on your coast,
East Sea!

That for five thousand years,
No, from the dividing of earth and sky,
Your mute but unfailing care
Has fostered this peninsula,
My beloved country.

Your blue dreams that heave and roll
And your sometimes tumultuous spirit
Have given us rugged mountains
And rivers and fields.
And you have kept watch over this indigent nation
Nestled in your domain.

East Sea! Nurturing mother of my country!
You lie today under a veil of cloud and mist,
Heavy with anxiety over the calamity engulfing this land.

To a Dead United Nations Soldier

Sitting at rest, say, beside a battery
During a brief lull in a battle desperate and fierce,
You may have reflected
On the bare landscape and meager assets of this country called
      Korea
And the unfortunate lot of its people.
And, yearning for the wife and children you left behind in your
      country far away,
To whom you might never return,
You reflected on your hopes for mankind and on yourself
      waging deadly battles in the name of justice.
God approved of your good resolution.
The day your family is notified of your death,
Your wife and children, who've been yearning for your return,
Will sink into a bitter chaos of sorrow and despair.
Your wife, whose heart is pierced with sorrow's eternal arrow,
Will tell your starry-eyed children morning and night
About your noble valor,
And delineate your beloved form, no longer to be met on earth.
They will pray for this small country in Asia
And be grateful God didn't forsake it to its doom.
How hateful that this atrocious war should make not only our
      people suffer
But also claim the lives of those not born on this land,
Sowing seeds of sorrow in the hearts of their loving families!
We shall remember your noble friendship in the name of mankind
And our hatred will be fierce and bitter
Toward the enemy who perpetrated this iniquity.

Port of Glory

Port city of Pusan!
I must sing of you.
In the year nineteen hundred and fifty,
When our nation's fate hung precariously on our flagpole's tip,
You saved it almost single-handedly.
This was the year of your glory.
The indigo skirt of the vast Pacific
Gently caresses your bosom.
I climb a plateau lined with poplars
And see the port bordered by a row of ships
Bearing friendship and aid from all over the world
To relieve our unfortunate land.
Black, yellow, copper, gray, cream,
The ships adorn the port like dishes on an offering table.
Weapons of all kinds are hauled ashore continuously
And soldiers with various hair colors wearing many kinds of caps
        pour out.
Countless refugees carrying pots and pans
Drift in the wake of a government which hopes to make you a
        springboard
To vault over the thirty-eighth parallel.
You were so overloaded your deck slanted
And waves lapped your stern,
So precarious was this ship called Korea!
But your fortitude restored its trim
In nineteen hundred and fifty.
You, the lever that lifted the country out of disaster!
Pusan, Port of Glory.

Glory Be to the Dutch Flag Forever

To the memory of Major Den Audin

Because you loved your own country
You couldn't stand to see
Another country unjustly trampled.

Your ancestors woke early from the ignorance of the Middle Ages,
And found their way to the part of the Orient
Still mired fast in medieval slumber.
You are a descendant of those valiant pioneers
Who brought us civilization's lamp.

You were as brave in defending another's land
As you were in loving your own country.
As a testament to your noble will

You held Korea in your last embrace.
Freedom and friendship will blossom from this earth wet with
          your crimson blood.

Far from cannon roar and gunpowder smoke,
Windmills turn peacefully in the west wind
On the banks of Zuider Zee in your country.
Carefully tended hyacinths and tulips dance in the rich fields
And your spirit, home at last, smiles up at your peaceful blue sky.
Your support and your brave ancestors' noble spirit
Will live in the blood of Korean people.
May glory and bliss be with your country forever!

Cleansing a Territory with the Enemy's Blood

On the day of the recapture of Seoul

If you capture the capital
Ten times through slaughter and carnage
Our soldiers, armed with righteousness,
Will take it back each time.

Look,
How the Han River flows as tranquilly as ever
After the gunsmoke has cleared,
And Pugak Mountain stands as loftily as before.
This is our precious capital
Founded by our ancestors long ago
And built up and tended by successive generations.
It is not a place we can relinquish to savages,
Even if they topple the lofty gates of our citadel,
Burn our bell towers down,
And singe the dwellings of our million inhabitants.
Our patriotic fervor will quickly build on the ruins
Broad avenues of peace and plenty
With timber and brick and tile.

Vicious fiends,
Your own blood will have to cleanse away
Your crimes against this sacred capital
Each time you capture and trample on it.

A *Counteroffensive*

The trigger of fury
That was pulled taut
Has been released.
Look.
Crusaders for justice rush in like angry waves,
Crossing the Naktong and Hyŏngsan rivers
And landing at the ports of Inch'ŏn, Kunsan and Samch'ŏk.
The cruel wolves
Who were tearing up the land and devouring their brethren
Are driven away like fallen leaves in autumn gales.
Don't let the fiends Kim Ilsung, Park Hŏnyŏng and Mu Chŏng
Escape unpunished.
Bash in their heads and crush their feet
Before they cross the Yalu.

It is fall.
The roar of cannons shakes
Heaven and earth.
Ah, we must pursue the enemy
Fiercely, like a storm.

Reeds

As if I'd drifted to Algeria or some such exotic place,
No friendly face greets me with a smile.
Pushed and shoved by millions
From P'yŏngan-do, Seoul, Hamgyŏng-do and Kangwon-do,
I drink grog, sitting on a piece of plank
In an eatery that has neither roof nor screen.
Gulls fly overhead.
This port city simmers with the greatest confusion of this century.
"Where are you from?" I ask the proprietor.
Wherever he's from,
He's a Korean and my compatriot.
The bushy-bearded proprietor, his wife and young children
Are so dirty and ragged that you can't guess at their ages.
I am their only customer today.

Gulls fly overhead,
Motorboats hum on the sea.
The sun glides over the island on the horizon.
People are exhausted
And charity has drained out of them.
Millions hover about this darkening harbor
Like so many reeds
With hollow hearts, like strangers in a strange land.

At Christmas, 1950

Even on this night when all the world
Rejoices, telling stories told and retold for two millennia,
In the secluded valley at the battlefront
No meteor flashes, heralding peace.
Only fighter bombers wail their steely resolution
Above roofs jolted by howling west wind.

You, my patiently suffering babes
Who drink water to soothe your hunger
But go to sleep without blaming your father,
You are the good angels of the twentieth century.
You judge with your young wisdom
What is just and what is not.

Mankind is headed for destruction.
So what if a sick poet starves in the street,
If the street in which a poet starves is sick?

Drifters

Look at the crowd of people
Thronging like a tangled heap of rubbish
On this street brushed by the cold waves of winter solstice.
The men have left behind pride and shame and attachment
And are offering for sale anything that will fetch a few pennies:
Their cherished furniture, clothing, shoes,
Even their wives' underwear.

Oh, do not talk of human sublimity
Or deplore human baseness.
What's left is only the primitive animal instinct to survive.

Above a street brushed by cold waves
The winter sky is high and clear.
But human hearts beneath are dark and sad.
They have sold their last scrap of pride,
And abandoned the homes of their fathers.
They will go anywhere,
To preserve lives tough as the soles of shoes.

Where to Go?

Emerging from the lean-to pleasantly drunk,
"Good bye,"
"God speed,"
We say, but I have no destination.

Standing outside the shoulder-high hut,
I look up at the sky that stretches over six continents,
Hangs over Tyrol, Tibet, and Brazil,
Places I often yearned to see.
But I have no true destination.

In these degenerate streets
Rotting with greed and selfishness,
No one cares about the future of the nation.
Here, where eating and dressing are shameless acts,
My raggedness doesn't bother me.

On the twigs of the few trees at the end of the street
Peach blossoms bloom, like remnants of affection,
And a light fog hovers.
How grateful I am for faithful spring!

My Fatherland

*On reading an interview on the Korean War
written by a foreign correspondent*

You wrote that there's no other country in the world
Whose land is so covered with festering sores,
Where the stench of excrement assails you wherever you go,
Where every creature to ever plague mankind thrives—
Flea, bedbug, mosquito, centipede, venomous snake, leech—
Whose people are
Pickpockets, swindlers, beggars, corrupt officials or scoundrels.
You say this country's worse than New Guinea,
A country you'd like to hand over to the enemy as punishment.
You ask, "What crimes have we committed that we have to fight
        for a country like this?"

I am a beggar child of that country.
I stay by its side
And weep over it all the time.

At the Combat Front

1.

In this shady spot in a field near a highway, beside the Ch'ŏng-cho Lake along whose thirty-*li*-long shore bullets fly and gunfire blazes between our soldiers and the enemy, moans of abuse, curses and furious yells reverberate.

An evening glow pregnant with instant death spreads with deceptive peace, and tracer bullets weave in and out of sorghum leaves like gorgeous ribbons. I hug the ground, serpent-like, and a stealthy bullet swishes by like a whisper, scattering mulberry leaves above my head. Bullets shower the bean leaves right before my eyes.

2.

My invisible enemy invidiously takes aim at me from all around. What is it they want?

These limbs and this body of mine?

3.

I don't feel a twinge of hatred or fury toward the enemy. On the contrary, my thoughts spread like ripples on a pond.

In this perilous spot where a tiny shift in the enemy's aim could blow up this body of mine, I focus on myself.

4.

What does the enemy really want from me?

My life?

My life is nothing more than a hypothesis maintained by agreement between my body (let's call it that for now) and me. So, I really don't know whose this body that I call mine really is.

At any rate, neither he who made the mulberry leaves scatter above my head nor he who fired the bullets that showered on the bean leaves before my eyes seems to have been its master.

5.

Therefore, if, at some time, an absolute being suddenly appeared and insisted on his right to my body, my agreement with my body would be cancelled and that hypothesis called my life would be sucked into the void with the whirl of a wounded dragonfly, and what would remain on this spot of earth would be...

6.

So, my groaning enemy, is it this body that you ridiculously want from me?

When that time comes, I will be stored securely in the treasure-house of eternity and won't be here.

At the Armistice Line

God!
How can we call Your attention to our plight?

After the earth convulsed and the ocean raged
And innumerable lives met bloody, atrocious deaths,
The mountains, clouds, trees and time recovered their repose,
But behind their vacant stillness
Demonic men are honing hatred and weapons of death.
Is this because evil spirits have entered their bellies, just as in the
          Bible they entered the bellies of swine?

This moment calls for Your intervention,
And cannot end without Your final judgment.
Are You holding back because it's still too early for You to step in?
Are You standing by letting humans commit these iniquities
So their final repentance will be stark?

God!
Do You remain aloof to make us grovel and supplicate?
God, why are You swaying nonchalantly on a blade of grass
          shaking in the breeze of noon?
God, how can You rest easily each night in Ursa Major?

from
Poetry on Burnt Ground
by Ku Sang
■

1.

Behind the tiny windowpane
Of the squatter's hut
Children's faces hang, like blazing sunflowers.

The faces withdraw, dazzled by the sun.
I, too, turn away.
My tearful shadow trudges behind me.

Turning into an alley, I halt.
Forsythias in bud
Peep from a heap of ashes near a hedge.

The little girl running down yonder hill
Is missing her front teeth,
Her smile innocent of the least taint of guilt.

I become content, like a drunk.
My shadow smiles as it leads the way.

2.

Who wouldn't smile to see someone coddling an octopus blackened by its own ink?

But my face stiffened, sitting opposite a black boy and his mother.

"My dear! Please don't fret. I'll ask your Daddy to buy you lots of candy!"

The pale-faced woman begs and pleads, trying to placate the black boy.

In the night train, the eyes of the tired passengers clearly show annoyance, and the dark head of the fretting boy and his fair-skinned mother's sweat-soaked forehead shine.

Embarrassed by the contorted faces of the mother and child, I rummage in my pocket for the box of caramel my friend gave me to chew on the journey and give it to the boy.

The effect is instantaneous. Blinking eyes darker than obsidian, he snatches the box, tosses a caramel into his mouth, and recovers his dignity.

After tossing in the second, third, and fourth caramel, he climbs into my lap and smiles at me, baring teeth whiter than quartz.

How could I push him away? I take him from his tearfully apologetic mother and entertain him like I once did a monkey in a zoo, bribing him with candies.

Then the unspeakable: after blankly gazing at me and the boy for a while, the tired woman drops off to sleep, and the child which had been so fretful also falls asleep in my lap, panting.

Having become the black boy's daddy by all appearance, I, too, close my eyes, with ineffable thoughts in my heart.

I think of the few dollar bills that must have brought him into being.

Could his father have died in battle and been buried on a hill of this land? Or could he have returned to his country with proud decorations?

On the tired and abandoned face of the woman I see all of us.

Hugging the innocent life breathing more peacefully now, I shudder at the futility that is human destiny.

The train shoots through the darkness and the passengers have all fallen asleep. Only I, thrust into the part of a black child's daddy, sweat.

3.

An icy Siberian wind
Whips the frozen earth of my heart.
In the rubbish heap
On a field of dried and tangled weeds

There are gaping cans, ration boxes with knocked-out bottoms,
Torn *Stars and Stripes*, broken bottles,
And the corpse of a puppy shot to death.
On a furrow cut by tank tracks
The stiff, dry carcass of a cat.

In front of a tent that looks like a vinyl hothouse
Blood-stained pants are drying
On a wire fence.
Pacing inside the fence
A yankee soldier whistles.
Then, from a hole in the ground,
Girls peep out, like groundhogs in spring,
Their heads wrapped with colorful scarves.

Vultures from out of nowhere
Streak the sky
And fly over the lowering mountain,
Foaming darkly at the mouth.

Oh, this intolerable itch on my skin!
This nausea that rises from my bowels!
What has triggered them?

4.

Scene I

Urchins on the road rush to a woman in garish garb and sur-
round her. One throws a stone at her, others smear her with horse
and cow dung stuck to the tips of rods.

"Western broad!" "Yankee broad!" "Yankee whore!"

The boys are trying her desecrated maternity with their own
law.

"What if I am a Yankee broad? I'm not your mother!"

A Yankee passing in a Jeep picks up the woman yelling and kicking at the boys and disappears like the wind. Leaving behind futile yells and taunts.

Scene II

A heavily-made-up woman in Western garb passes by. Little boys wink at each other.

One boy steals up to her back and pins a paper tag to her blouse.

"On sale for three thousand *won*."

"Hahaha." "Hahaha." "Hahaha!"

The boys laugh their laugh of contempt and self-derision, conscious that they can do nothing to negate her existence.

The woman checks her outfit and tries to walk more straight.

But the urchins continue their laugh until she disappears from view.

"Hahaha." "Hahaha." "Hahaha!"

Scene III

Soon darkness descends on the back street, and the urchins leave off playing and begin looking for passers-by.

When black and white drunken soldiers appear, they grab their powerful arms with their small hands.

"Hello, Girl Okay." "Nice Madam!" "Pretty Chicks."

Little urchins, having discovered the power of money, bow to it.

7.

At the cemetery of enemy soldiers

The souls lying here in neat rows
Won't be able to rest.

We were firing at you until yesterday,
But we culled your bones with those very hands
And buried you carefully,

Choosing a sunny plot on this secluded hill,
And planted grass on the mounds as well.
Death has the mysterious power
To make us transcend love and hate.

If your souls try to return to your hometowns
You'll be blocked by mountains before you go thirty *li*.
The silence of the mountain, owned by neither side,
Weighs on my heart
Like tons of iron.

We were bound to you in life
By ties of hate.
But now, your lingering resentments
Are my responsibility
And are incorporated in my prayers.

In the spring sky overhead
A leisurely cloud
Drifts toward the North.
I burst into tears
Before this grave of dear enemies
At the sound of cannon in the distance.

8.

Lord, whisper to me
Always
Even in this hellish din.

Reveal yourself to me
Through the phantoms and rainbows that flit before my eyes.

Give me a blade of grass

To cover the shameful nakedness of my body.
My songs are of your love.
Let me call your name until my tongue wears out.

Give me Noah's ark
In the coming flood of fire;

But let me be with the young lambs
That fall like petals.

9.

At the time of the armistice negotiations

My fatherland! You are pitiful as Sim Ch'ŏng, sold as sacrifice to
    redeem her blind father's pledge.
The poet grows tearful when he calls your name.
All the butchers of this century
Are going to carve you up, like a piece of meat.
Heaven seems to just look on.

My Fatherland! On your streets people go mad,
Unable to hope or even to despair.
Your enemy and the enemy's patrons
Are trying to slice you up again.
Are you a reed that gets mowed down, thinking?

My Fatherland! Country of resentful ghosts!
Your only constant companion
Has been calamity.
Once again your trusting and threadbare children
Are shaking their fists at Panmumjŏm
With desperate fury and anxiety.
But we hear no song to console the dead souls.

My Fatherland! Pitiful as Sim Ch'ŏng, an offering to propitiate
        the sea god!
My Fatherland!

10.

Streams of spring,
Wash away all our sordid Karma,
Which has been growing like snowballs.

This spring,
Let us all sow seeds of life
On this ruin
Where the bones of glory and disgrace alike have been charred.

Even if the sky falls and the earth collapses
Suddenly one morning,
I shall cling to life.

I have no expectations
For tomorrow.
But our great yearning for life
Is stronger than fate.

Let us plant seeds of life,
Lovingly, joyfully,
So that they will bloom on our graves
And testify to our resurrection.

from
Unforgettable People
by Yu Ch'un-do
■

Destiny

I go to the outpatients clinic with my assignment slip.
Yesterday's wounded ROK soldiers are nowhere in sight,
And only a doctor and a nurse pace the empty room.
Jeeps carrying wounded soldiers arrive
In the hospital yard.

Some are carried in on stretchers, some hobble in leaning on others,
And some hop in on one leg.
Beyond the window, the sight is the same as yesterday's,
Except they have red stars on their caps and a stronger odor
        of sweat.
The doctor and the nurse do the same things they did yesterday.
Is that the spirit of the Red Cross?

Our destiny of partings, death, and imprisonment
Began that day.
The bitterness of many decades lay in wait.

"I Love You, Comrade"

When you're past seventy and you feel death drawing near,
All of life's fluff vanishes from memory like chaff in the wind,
And the truth of life that you had hidden deep inside
Soars up, like fireflies
In the darkness.

Tracing my way to the past along memory lane,
I follow the gleam of a fragment of memory
Which surfaced from oblivion's valley.
I collect slices of time
To piece together the scattered puzzle
And print the undeveloped negatives which lay buried.

I hear the secret whisper of my being
Emerging from shards of memory.

Where is he?
Where is the man who marched off to a deadly battlefield?
Is he still limping along a valley
In the back hills of this continuing history of division,
Dragging his wounded leg?
Is he climbing a slope in the snow,
His leg still in pain,
Crossing a barbed wire fence?

What did he thirst after,
While he hovered on the brink of death?
What did the man of steel yearn for in his heart?

It lasted only five minutes,
But the light of his burning eyes
Stayed with me for fifty years.

The seed of compassion I could not give him sprouted in sorrow
And blossomed into a flower of love in my heart.

Where is he?
If he is alive and we meet again,
I will return him a clear answer:
"Comrade, I love you, too."

The Girl Soldier and the Moon

The highway stretched endlessly to the north
Under the pale moon.
Poplar trees lined the road, both sides
Dense with foliage.

On the moon-blanched highway
A girl soldier spurred on three oxcarts loaded with wounded men,
Disturbing the pebbles.

The pale moon peeked out through the clouds
As if to watch over the girl.

Suddenly, a rumbling sound came
From the southern sky
And two airplanes appeared.
The pale moon tried to duck behind the clouds
To hide the oxcarts from view,
But the planes overtook them like lightning.

Like eagles swooping down on their prey,
The planes spewed bombs.
The pale moon looked down
Fretting helplessly.

The oxcarts were overturned
And the wheels spun nosily in the air.
The wounded, spilled from the carts, died, their blood staining
        the highway red.

The moon clicked its tongue in pity
And moaned.

After a while, the girl stood up, wiped her tears,
And began to plod north alone,
Looking back at her comrades again and again.

Looking up at the moon, the girl asked,
"Why do they bomb us?
This land is ours!"
The pale moon answered,
"How would I know?"

The Emergency Field Hospital

Cannons boom with a terrible rumble from afar
And rays of blue light streak the pitch-black night sky.
Screams from the emergency field hospital
Rip the night.
The wounded brought in today are in surgery.
I call up the pale, childlike face
Of a young soldier.
Piercing screams shake the night several times
Then sink into the darkness.

I envision the young soldier's leg
Being cut off without anesthesia.
I bury my face in my hands
But the poor boy's leg looms before my eyes.
Tears streak down my cheeks.

Someone says urgently, "Comrade, we need your help."
"Oh, they want me," I think
And, pushing aside a sliding door with torn paper panels,
I rush out into the dark yard.
A messenger stinking of sweat is waiting for me.
"I'm coming, comrade," I say,
And run after the messenger
To the improvised operating room.
The military doctor lifts a corner of the black sheet
That shields the room from sighting by planes
And tiredly mutters through his gauze mask,
"Please help us, comrade,"
Without looking at me.
In the dim light, his face is green with fatigue and anxiety.

The young soldier whose his leg was amputated without anesthesia
faints and is carried out on a stretcher.

The dark sheet is lowered again and everything is engulfed in
      darkness once more. The cannon sounds louder and closer.
Cold and fear grip me. My feet wobble with the accumulated
      fatigue of many days as I follow the stretcher. I clench my
      teeth and keep walking.
"Isn't this all a nightmare?" I ask myself.
The bearers take the soldier on the stretcher to the infirmary.

The whole village was empty. We occupied the biggest house and
      made it an emergency field hospital.
Although called a hospital, it was no more than an infirmary.
The wounded arrived in endless streams
And we were out of anesthetic by afternoon.
We operated on urgent cases
By tying the limbs of the wounded to the bed
And knocking them out.
Cannons boom nearer and louder.
I feel the pulse of the young soldier.
His faint breathing indicates that he is alive.
I gaze down at his face, pale as death.
Why, oh why, should there be this war?

The face of my younger brother in Pusan, who is about this young
      soldier's age, flits before my eyes.
I shudder and shake off the thought that he might be aiming his
      gun at us as a soldier of the Republic.
This is a nightmare. This must be a nightmare.
Later I cross the dark yard toward the emergency operating room.
Cannons rumble nearer still.

Maggots

Unable to suppress my nausea
I rush out of the room.
I take a few deep breaths
And return.
Maggots crawled out of the wound on the soldier's leg,
Covering his whole leg in white
While I was away.

Hundreds, thousands, of maggots crawl out
And spread everywhere.
I stand as though paralyzed.
The soldier's unfocused eyes
Gaze absently at the maggots
Crawling out of his wound and up his body.

Biting my lip hard,
I scoop maggots from the wound
With all the cotton I have
And pour disinfectant into it.
My throat makes a hoarse sound
As I try to suppress sobs.

I look at the soldier's face.
He looks like a boy still in his teens.
His innocent eyes
Just gaze into the void.
Tears gush out of my eyes
And I wrap his head in my hands and arms.

The soldier's unfocused eyes
Still gaze into the void.

Namgang River

In the pitch darkness, the crossing to death begins.
The first batch. Then the second. Then the third.
The soldiers begin
Their journey of no return,
Holding their guns straight up to heaven.

Reconnaissance planes circle overhead.
The river gleams with a silvery sheen.
A fighter bomber appears, then another, then another.
Napalm bombs fall in a shower of flames.
Blood spreads on the river
And the water turns the color of earth.
Bodies flow downstream.

"You must live.
Return to the rear.
There will be no more wounded for you to treat,"
The young commander says to me solemnly.
Exhorting me to hold life sacred, he steps into his own death.

Then
He begins to cross the river of no return,
Leading soldiers who will not return,
Who will dye the river red.

Oh, you grass on the banks of Namgang River!
You who will feed on the blood of these soldiers!
Remember this day forever more!

Kŭmgang River Ghost

Like a senseless fool, I closed my eyes
And silently counted to three.
I flopped down on the ground,
All strength drained out of me.
But no bullet struck,
And someone grabbed my hand and helped me up.

I'm not even hurting.
I can't believe I'm alive. I open my eyes to see where I am.
Beside the soldier of the Republic
Who had aimed his gun at me
Stands an American soldier,
His face caked with dust.
In my dim consciousness I hear the American ask the Korean soldier,
"Why are you shooting at this girl?"
The flustered Korean soldier replies,
"Communist, Communist," pointing at me.
I recover my senses instantly,
And see a path opening toward life.
I shout, "No, no! I'm a student!"

The soldier who aimed his gun at me and said, "Now you're a
          ghost of this river"
Took a step backward, with a resigned face.
Sitting on the front bumper of the Jeep driven by the American G.I.,
I shed tears of relief,
Saved from becoming a ghost of the Kŭmgang River.
But I was transported to Ch'ŏngju Prison not long afterward
With numerous Communist soldiers who looked much like me.

Let's Take Our Own Lives

Emitting bizarre screams
The G.I. romps and stomps
Circling the row of prisoners
Like one gone stark mad
Or a monkey in heat.

He jabs the rumps of male prisoners
With the muzzle of his gun,
Or pulls the ponytails
Of female prisoners.

The yells and screams grow wilder
As he dances around the female prisoners.
Up on the hill beyond
A half-naked G.I. spews obscenities
And bares his bleached-looking body.

My terrified heart turns somersaults in my chest,
And my hand grabbing the hand of the girl in front of me
Is wet with cold sweat.

I bite my lip to still my tremors
And a taste of blood spreads in my mouth.

"Mother, what's going to become of me?"
My mother's anxious face
Passes before my eyes.

Suddenly, fury pushes up from my belly,
And the pounding in my heart is stilled.
I recover my icy will.
I squeeze my comrade's hand
And say,

"Let's take our own lives.
Kill ourselves before they defile us."

Tears flow out of the women prisoners' eyes
As they nod assent.
Are they tears of fury or of sorrow?
Are they thinking of their parents?

To us, then,
Only death was our friend and savior
And the source of our courage.

Acting as their eldest sister,
I ask for the commanding officer in my broken English,
And we were sent to Ch'ŏngju Prison unharmed.

That tall girl
Who walked with me grasping my hand tightly.
Is she alive today?

And the young nurse
Whose large, fearful eyes
Were always wet with tears.
Is she still alive?

In Ch'ŏngju Prison

Into Ch'ŏngju Prison
Lit up brightly
Scores of American military trucks
Are carrying
Captured DPRK soldiers.

The prisoners' faces are wretched
With terror and hunger.
Their eyes are sunken,
Their cheeks haggard,
All their features seem shriveled, except cheekbones.

All of them are wearing
White jackets and trousers,
Which make them look like a defeated athletic team.

Before the tall American guard
The Korean KATUSA is hitting his brother--enemies
With the barrel of his gun
And yelling,
"All Red chicks should be done in."

Tetanus spreads among the prisoners.
The flustered Americans create an infirmary
And let DPRK army doctors and women prisoners treat the patients.

There is no vaccine and no medicine.
All we can do is to sterilize the wound
And sprinkle antibiotic powder.
The infirmary's filled with the stench of rotting flesh.

Unable to shut their mouths, the tetanus patients drool.
Their jaws locked,

They can neither talk nor eat
But only wait for death.

My professor at the medical school
Said that once you see the face of a tetanus patient
It remains printed in your memory.

Yes, this is what happens in a war,
And this war is wrong, I thought.

American trucks
Bring in prisoners
Day and night.
More prisoners die of tetanus.

One day I meet a brother of my friend
In the prison.
"Why are you here?" he asks in amazement.
He fetches an American officer.
With his help, I am released
And escape death once more,
Incredibly.

In those days
You lived if you were lucky
And died if you were not.
My heart aches still
When I think of those days.

The wretched faces of tetanus patients
Who were patient and submissive
In the face of death.
The terrified grip of the young female prisoner
Who held my hand like a vise
As she fell asleep.

The faces of Communist army doctors
Lit by the bonfires
They built in the yard of the infirmary
To guard the female prisoners
From intruders.
Faces I cannot forget.

I left them behind,
Escaped alone,
Lived fifty years.
But I will never escape
The guilt and the pain
That always clings to me
Wherever I go.

Crickets Chirping in My Ear

When the detective approached her
With a water kettle and a white cloth,
Kiltae screamed and fell into a fit,
Fainting on the spot.
The man winced a little,
Then spat,
Muttering, "Tough bitches!"
And cut me with a glance.
I felt the blood drain from my face,
And my heart thrashed in my chest.

One of my ears went deaf during the previous night's "interrogation,"
And a thousand crickets began chirping in that ear.
I'm going deaf, I thought.
But that'll be a problem only if I live.
I envied Kiltae her fainting fit.

The man left, slamming the door,
Perhaps judging that he'd given us enough for the day.
I stood there like one gone out of her wits,
Looking down at unconscious Kiltae.

The man returned and led us back to our cell,
Our limbs bound tight with ropes.

Those crickets have been chirping in my ear
For fifty years.
They will accompany me to my grave.

The Female Guerrilla

to Mrs. Chŏng Sundŏk, in her hospital room

In the dark and strange hospital cell
The stump of her body rolls this way and that.
She lost her husband and one leg
In snow-covered Mt. Chiri valley.
She later lost an arm
And her remaining leg
But she's survived for forty years.

Alas, alas! The curse of our nation fell heavily on her.
Only eyes, throat, and an arm remain,
But her spirit is undaunted nevertheless.
Waving her only limb,
She shouts, "I'm alive, alive,
Thanks to the love of my comrades."

Her eyes are shining and dry.
She buried all her tears
In the grave of her husband on snow-covered Mt. Chiri.

Bouyed by the support of her comrades,
She disdains self-pity.
She lives on their love;
And if life proves a dream,
She'll find her true home with her husband
On snow-covered Mt. Chiri, where her dead comrades
        will welcome her with dance and song.

Mo Yun-suk

■

What the Dead Soldier Said

*While wandering over the hills of Kwangju I saw a soldier
of the Republic of Korea lying dead, alone.*

I see a dead soldier
Lying alone in a deserted valley.
Neither stirring nor uttering a word
The soldier lies facing the sky, eyes closed.

The shining insignia on your brown uniform
Tells me you were a lieutenant of the proud ROK army.
Warm blood still gushes from your chest.
Your blood is more fragrant than the scent of a rose.
I prostrate myself on the ground, weeping for you,
And listen to your last words:

I ended my life at twenty-five.
I died a son of the Korean Republic.
I fought many long and fierce battles
Guarding the hills of my country
From the deadly hordes of invading enemies.
Armed with an invincible gun in my hand
And unbreakable helmet on my head,
I was never a coward before my enemy.
I repulsed the enemy
Running through hills and valleys and tombs and brambles
Like Admiral Yi Sun-shin, Napoleon, and Caesar,
Driven by the spirit of Taehan in my blood.
Night and day I marched forward
To save my country from peril.

I wanted to push on
Beyond the enemy lines
And clear the sky of this storm

All the way to the horizon.

I had a mother and father
And dear brothers and sisters.
I had a lovely sweetheart.
I wanted the happiness of youth
And a life among friends and neighbors
In my hometown.
I wanted to grow and sing
With the numberless birds
Taking wing freely in my country's skies.
That's why I fought bravely
And fighting, died.
No one will know of my death,
But my beloved fatherland!
Tender breezes gently dry the beads
Of perspiration on my dead face,
And the blue stars in the sky
Keep me company all night long.

Snug in my country's uniform
I take a pleasant rest in this grassy glade.
I rest my tired body awhile
Drinking in the air wafting through the sky.
To have fought for my mother country
Is my pride,
And to have died for it
Is my glory.
Lying here in this nameless valley
Soaking in the night dew,
I have become a companion
Of the invisible nightingale.

Ah, wind! And you nameless birds!
If, in your wanderings

You chance to meet my suffering compatriots,
Please tell them
Not to cry for me but to cry for my fatherland.
You, bird of spring.
If you meet my lovely sweetheart by a window
In one of your aerial flights,
Tell her not to cry
For longing of me
But to cry for our sacred country.

My fatherland! My compatriots!
And you, my beloved sweetheart!
I gave my life for your happiness.
See that the enemy is repulsed
So that my youth will not have been cut short in vain.

To retreat is cowardice.
More so than surrender or slavery.
Even if all our allies retreat,
You, soldiers of the Korean Republic!
You must fight on this land.
You must die for this land.
A fatherland once forsaken
Cannot be yours again.
Heed the coming storm, Republic of Korea!
Wolves and lions are crossing the mountains and rivers.
Our beloved brothers
Are leaving for exile to faraway Siberia.
Are you going to close your eyes to all this?
You mustn't stand by, calling it fate.
What if it is fate?
We are stronger than fate.
Friends! Shatter this Fate imposed by our enemy.
With your strong arms and legs,
Your red blood, and the dauntless spirit of Tangun,

You must fight your battles and die your deaths
To breathe life into our dying nation.

I gladly forego a grave for my body
Or even a small coffin to shield me from wind and rain.
Soon, rough winds will whip my body
And worms will feast on my flesh,
But I will gladly be their companion.
My ardent wish is to become a handful of earth
In this valley in my fatherland
Waiting for better times for my brethren.

I see a dead soldier
Lying alone in a deserted valley.
Neither stirring nor uttering a word
The soldier lies facing the sky, eyes closed.

The shining insignia on your brown uniform
Tells me you were a lieutenant of the proud ROK army.
Warm blood still gushes from your chest.
Your blood is more fragrant than the scent of a rose.
I prostrate myself on the ground, weeping for you,
And listen to your last words.

Chang Ho-gang
■

A Hymn to a Comrade

You grab the M-1 rifle like you did your hoe.
Your posture as you crouch in a firing trench
Shows you are a farmer.

Even the stars have fallen asleep,
But your eyes pierce the darkness
Sharp as a cat's,
Like when you watched for thieves in your watermelon shed.
Your tanned skin, your mouth clamped shut,
Your broad nose, your sleepless eyes,
And your body, hard and tense as iron, are all throbbing with fire.

You swallow lumps of frozen rice dipped in red pepper paste
On this ridge raining with shells,
And then peacefully exhale cigarette smoke.
How trustworthy you look!

When battle begins, you rush at the enemy
Hurling hand grenades with a furious yell.
Did you study trajectory in your childhood
When you fought stone wars over the village brook?

Cooking rice with snow collected in a lunchbox
On New Year's Day,
You said you realized the magnitude of your mother's love.

Ah, you are a brave Flower Youth!
A friend of liberty!
You will find genuine peace,
You will win true victory,
Because your love is true.

Though the shells of the fiends
Shower all around me,
Though I stand in the line of enemy fire,
I have my wits about me
Because you smile at me.

If it hadn't been for your constant and pious prayer,
How could I stride along
The edge of the sharp ridge wrapped in mist
And the valley strewn with mines
From which the signs have disappeared?

We must carry our Fatherland on our back.
Because I have your support
And your love,
My veins throb with fire
Even in the trench noisy with exploding shells,
And I am ready for a million Communists.

If I Fall

If I fall while fighting
On a nameless ridge
Before we achieve unification

Let not my comrades cover my body with wildflowers.
Don't drape the Republic's flag on my bleeding chest.
You needn't list any inheritance for my children,
Or bury me in a grave and mark the spot.

No one would care much
If, after foxes and crows picked off my flesh, you inscribed on my
        skull,
"This man died before his wish
Of drinking a sip of water from the Ch'ŏnji Lake
Was fulfilled,"
In the most elegant calligraphy.

My skull,
After rolling along the Taebaek Mountains,
Breaking and shattering against every peak
Until it becomes fine powder,
Will be whisked away like snowflakes by a wind blowing north
        one day
And dropped on Ch'ŏnji Lake where it will sink into the depth
        of ages.

Kansas Line

Since you have the map of Korea spread before you
Why don't you draw a line on the overlay with an oil pencil?

Who named the 230-kilometers-long combat front
Stretching from Taejin-po on the east coast, 38.5 degrees North
      Latitude
Past Kŏnbong Pass, Hyangro Peak, Ŭngbong Mountain, Magpie
      Peak, the Ridge of Blood, the Hwach'ŏn Dam,
Beyond the Iron Triangle, along the Imjin River and ending at the
      Yellow Sea
The Kansas Line?

Here, in the mid-east region where the Soyang and Pukhan rivers
      flow weeping,
And hills and peaks pierce the blue heavens,
And the savage north wind that whipped the earth like a terrorist
Bounces off to the Punchbowl Basin after smashing the slope of
      Tae-ŏm Mountain,
And the dark clouds that heaved and rolled sigh and divide
When blocked by Sorak Mountain,
And streams and bogs run deep enough to wet the earth's core,

We dig, build, install, and bury
Firing trenches, shelter trenches, wire fences, and mines
In a tight network
So that even a swarm of enemies skilled in night maneuvers
Couldn't penetrate our defense,
Even by burrowing underground like moles.

Behold! The wings of fury
Flying toward the north day and night.
Flames spewed out by rockets
And the muzzles of recoilless guns and howitzers

Consume the sky, earth, forest, streams, pebbles
And the skulls of enemies.
A meteor may streak the sky
But all eyes are riveted on the North.

Tonight, after pillars of napalm fire have subsided
And the moon and stars weep,
The soldier's heart flies to his hometown in the North,
Which abounds in legends.
Ah, who drew this Kansas Line
That keeps the strong spirits of soldiers
From ranging freely?

The Armistice Line at Night

from the diary of a soldier

The moonless night is blacker than death,
The quiet armistice line colder than the grave.
The young soldier's heart is bleak
On this long, frosty autumn night.

When a falling leaf borne on an autumn breeze
Brushes his helmet,
The eyes of the soldier waiting in ambush in the trench
Sharply pierce the forest on the slope.
"It's about time the bastards came creeping."

Sure enough, machine-gun fire pours into the sentry box on the
          right.
"What are they rutting out for, this time?"
Instantly, the soldier's mouth clamps shut
And his finger flexes on the trigger.

Who fired? A shell illuninates into the sky
Above where the tracer bullet flew,
Lighting up the void like a huge, luminous red lotus blossom.
"I see them. Under the wooden railings and beside the wire
          fence."
Soon the platoon leader's commands ring out.

Firing commences from the camps on the right and left.
Hand grenades, carbines, M1, AR, LMG, M79, grenade launchers,
          trench mortars.
The symphony of firearms never ceases.
Bloodshot eyes pierce the darkness;
Tense eardrums don't miss a sound.

A sentry issues a call for a medic.
"Who's injured?"
I shake all over
With fury and hatred,
But my finger is steady on the trigger.

Landmines sporadically convulse the earth
And xenon searchlights crisscross the sky.
"The bastards are fleeing into the rushes."
Instantly, our fire converges on the rushes
And the enemies' shrieks and screams soothe our ears.

After the platoon leader's commands thunderously rang out,
The sound of gunfire ceased.
"How many of the bastards did we get?" we wonder.
When the cold wind strikes our sweat-soaked uniforms,
The soldier without a watch asks,
"What time is it?"

Another meteor glides in silence.
When the chirping of insects evoke memories of home,
The soldier recalls the face of his beloved.
The Dipper, which had been in the bead of his northward-aiming
        rifle,
Has disappeared.

Dedicating a Flower

You fought bravely for our Fatherland,
Yet no medal adorned your breast.

You gave your arms, legs, and eyes,
And your body was bruised and torn,

But without a mite of regret
You made yourself an offering to liberty.

The flowers upon your grave
Have the color and fragrance of your blood.

Your meritorious service in the war
Should bring you glory and rewards.

But our hungry and threadbare country
Can give you nothing.

Even if you leave the perilous armed forces,
A troubled society awaits you.

Destroyed cities and ruined villages
Stand on denuded hills and valleys gone dry.

Even if the whole world laughs at you,
You still have your iron will in your heart.

Do not grieve over your maimed body and ruined home.
Grieve only if you have lost the will to rebuild your life and home.

May you plant flowers in your garden of tomorrow
And reap bouquets of joy in time!

Chang Su-ch'ŏl
■

In the Freezing Trench

The temperature falls below zero again
And my very marrow seems to freeze
As I stand in this dark trench
Aiming straight at the enemy.

Ah, how many times and how savagely we fought
To recapture that hill!
Yesterday and today
Shells exploded and the earth shook.

Though the enemy may rush at us
Like a pack of wolves,
Our iron will and eager young blood
Will vanquish all Communists.

My body and the gun in my hands
Throb with pride
For the times I smashed the enemy
And made victory songs resound.

Beyond that ridge
Lies my beloved hometown.
I yearn for my hometown's hills
More keenly when seasons change.
I weep, thinking of my hometown
And of my family moaning through the night
Shaking with dread
Under the enemy's evil hooves.

I will be there
And hold you to my bosom
Before spring comes and streams swell with melted snow.

I strengthened my resolve
Standing in this dark trench
Sharply watching out for the enemy
Without slackening my attention for a moment.

The temperature falls.
A star glides across the sky.
When will the trumpet blare
Calling me to lead the attack?

Kim Kwang-rim

■

April, Which Prepared for June

April
Is the reason
I came back from the war.

In April
The waking earth
Exhales mist.

And blind insects, allowed to look at the earth, raise their heads,
      lean on the frail legs of birds, and break out in song

Announcing the reason
The flowers dropped seeds.

The thriving palm and banana trees shudder from fatigue
Of husk and flesh, husk and flesh.

Now,
We build more bonfires on sand
In this hungry country.

It was June,
When bullets tore
The broken sky.
The footprints made by the trampling feet of June are strewn all
      over your flowerbed and mine.

June was the reason
I returned from the war,
For the slaughtered moonlit night and the babies who lost their
      mothers' breasts
In April.

Kim Kyu-dong

■

A Grave

No one knows how
The handsome boy who came down driving a tank,
Son of a fisherman in Hamkyŏng-do,
And Private First Class Kim,
Son of a farmer tilling the slope of Chiri Mountain,
Came to be buried
In a single grave.
Time passed
And the landscape changed,
But no guns salute these youthful dead,
No visitors come to offer flowers.
The weapons they carried
Have turned to dust.
Animals of all kinds
Come to frolic with their spirits
And clouds linger on the grave
Fondly, as in affectionate caress.

Private Kim leads the handsome boy
On a tour of the Chiri and Halla Mountains,
And the beautiful boy takes Private Kim
On an excursion through Mt. Paekdu, Kŭmkang, and the Kaema
          Heights.

Each draping his arm on the shoulders of his pal,
They bound over the Armistice Line
No living man can cross,
And they farm and fish together
With the sun and the moon as their companions.
The two young men from the south and the north
Are living freely, as equals,
Anywhere they like on the three thousand li
Of their unified fatherland.

I don't know who buried these two untimely dead
In a common grave
On this shabby slope
Overgrown with grass.
But whoever passes
Lingers beside the grave
And offers silent tribute
To the two young men
Who could confirm their brotherhood
Only after death.

Min Jae-shik

■

Scapegoats

> And the unclean spirits came out, and entered the swine; and the
> herd, numbering about two thousand, rushed down the steep bank
> into the sea, and were drowned in the sea. (Mark 5:13)

On a summer resort bejeweled with flowers
A confused world map is spread out.

Foam seethes on the Bering Strait,
Squeezed on both sides by hostile powers.

The hand of Alaska is gaunt and weak.
The horns of Kamchaka bristle.
And the protruding nose of Shantung Province
       looks menacingly red.
And my country—
My country which is an unforgettable song,
Shivers and cringes into a corner of the Pacific.

I see the pathos of lonely Oceanus
In the white smoke exhaled by silent smokers.
Though their hearts pound vigorously,
They have to think of death.
Youths have more agonies to bear than does corn,
(which has to grow a beard before its ears are formed).
On the slopes of denuded hills
Tired villages wriggle.

(Hills are wrinkles of the earth frowning at the pranks of men.)
The modest hopes of villagers
Will blow away like dandelion seeds, come destitute spring.

Discussions and arguments don't yield any conclusion.
Proposals pile up in the "Decisions deferred" box,

And powerful men from powerful countries
Haggle over Korea.

Even though born to a proud country,
What have we done to be proud of?
Though our hearts burn with tropical heat, our ardor bears no
        fruit.
And the sad youths have nothing more to talk about.

Is Korea a chip in the superpowers' poker game?
Are Koreans scapegoats?

We push open the windows
And look up at the sky.
A cloud floats across it lightly,
Weightless, insubstantial.

Mun Sang-myŏng

■

White Horse Hill

Oh, the battle of that day and night
Was savage enough to tear the heavens down.

Shells flashed and powder smoke raged in a tempest
Over the gorgeous autumn colors on White Horse Hill.

Here, without God's prophesy,
The two sides locked in battle more than thirty times.
A second turned into eternity:
Youth shattered.

Over four-hundred-thousand shells and bullets were fired
On this hill where the death agonies of innumerable soldiers
Consumed the mystery of eons
And lives fell like grass and twigs.
Ah, the blood that ran down the hill
In a flood!

But the command
Rolled us into one great flaming cannonball.
The pile of corpses made an altar,
And blood was offered in place of wine.
Who was it that named this hill of blood and fire
White Horse Hill?
The white horse galloped away
And only living ghosts wail.

What does injury, even death, matter?
Loyal youths bound over White Horse Hill
And rush to the AB ridge
To hurl themselves at the enemy.

The sky and the earth
Are both gloomy.
Would a white horse of peace come
To this cursed bit of land?
Will it really come?

Lost Time and Effaced Language

at the National Cemetery

In this valley where conversation has stopped,
And roses shrivel black,
So much meaning
And lost time,
And the effaced white language of the afternoon
Smile at my frozen heart.

Everywhere I see
Tombs of uniform appearance,
Dyed autumn leaves,
And bitterness that will linger forever.
It is too cold and cloudy
For souls to rest peacefully
In the national cemetery today.

In the midst of the dead
My lost youth,
Which is longer than a lifetime,
Lingers heavy as lead.

Nursing a gray sorrow
Which cannot find an outlet,
Unable even to hoot like an owl,
I walk among the silent rows
Of my comrades' pure souls.
But the one face that I yearn for
Remains hidden.

In this space where thought is aflame
The sun has lost heat,
Driving the pigeons home.

But the silent witnesses

To the wounds
Which nothing can heal
Keep their silence
Till the end of time.

The *Blackout Line*

We are standing on a battlefield
In our fatherland
Where, by day and by night,
As an act of supreme morality,
We must empty
Iron bullets mercilessly
Into the bosoms of other human beings
We now call "enemy."

This nameless ridge
Where countless young men
In the first bloom of youth
Fell, like so many crimson flowers,
We called "the Ridge of Blood."

The Blackout Line
Is drawn with a careless hand
Across the ridge.

You mustn't turn on the light!
Don't let the enemy
Spot a light
Even for a second.
Even the gleam
Of your luminous eyes
Should be hidden
From the enemy.

Taking a respite
Under the maple trees
After desperate combat,
We collect our breaths
And ponder the worth

Of the blackout line.

That's right.
The real enemies
Are those whose souls
Live in darkness.
They think and act without light.
If only they had the conscience
To love light,
I would be driving a golden carriage
Brimming with happy songs
Over this hill clad in autumn foliage,
Speeding toward the Diamond Mountains
Scattering laughter in the wind.

When we pass the blackout line
We must be silent
As corpses.
Our tanks must be camouflaged,
And none of us dare light
Even one cigarette.
This is a region
From which light has been extinguished.

I wish we could move the blackout line signs
To the entrance of their barracks
Where they naturally belong,
And smoke our fill of cigarettes
Till we drop off to sleep.

And if this hateful silence
More ominous than death
Continues,
Then I'll recall
The fair and light shoulders

Of my beloved,
Which heaved as she sobbed at our parting,
With her long hair streaming down her back.
My beloved
Whom I left
Among the singing crickets
On the hill behind my home.

Hush! An explosion!
Am I not allowed
Even a moment of happy reverie?
Must they shatter it unmercifully?

Shells explode continuously.
That's right.
The enemy must hate
Even the gleam of fancy in our eyes.

That's right.
Before we exterminate the enemy,
Let someone draw
In deep black
Another blackout line
On my charred and arrested heart.

I am a shabby Bohemian
Who, loathingly but dutifully,
Roams the battlefield
With the blackout line sign
Stuck in his throbbing heart.

Pak Il-song

■

War Diary

Even a whirlwind couldn't
Suck up so many lives.
Even a maelstrom couldn't
Swallow so many lives.

Exploding shells,
Cataclysmic convulsion of the earth.
"All hell breaking loose"
Aptly describes a place like this.

It's unbelievable that I'm alive.
I can't understand
How I can be here
Recalling that time
I should have died.

Do I owe it to my mother's prayer?
Every night she prayed for my safety,
Offering a bowl of pure water to mountain spirits.

To capture a hill from the enemy,
To take trenches on a ridge,
We had to create a sea of blood
More crimson than the evening glow.
Are lives something more resplendent
Than stars?

After a bout of combat,
Powder smoke and battle dust
Make up a flowerbed,
And petals blow in the wind.

It's better to be alive
Without eyes and arms,
And with broken legs.
But the comrades who do not answer our call:
Where can we find them?
How can we reach them?

The Eyes of the Sentry

The sentry
Standing in the rain
Saluted me
And I saluted back.
But, deeming it insufficient, he reports:

"On sentry duty. All clear."

You stare at a corner of the camp
With your piercing eyes.
Not even an ant
Would risk trying
Your vigilance.

Your eyes shine
More brightly than stars.
They're not the eyes
With which you looked up at your mother
While she fed you at her breast.
You were a gentle boy
In your hometown.
You flinched when a thorn pierced your finger.
But with a gun in your hand
Your eyes are fierce.

It is raining tonight
And so dark I can't even see my feet,
But your eyes are piercing.

The password is "Naktong River."
The water flows,
And our sad history
Is getting drenched.

Pak In-hwan
■

To My Baby Daughter

You were born amid the noise of machine guns and cannon fire.
You were born into a world of rampant death.
So, you are growing up a weak child,
And your cries are weak, too.

Your mother moved abode seven times in three months,
With you clasped in her bosom.
On the day blood rained in Seoul
And freezing cold attacked it with snow,
You rode south on the roof of a freight train
With scant clothes to shield you from the cold.

My baby daughter, growing up smiling even in the midst of pain,
Nurtured only on your mother's milk,
What do you yearn for in your inmost heart?

Your eyes, liquid as a blue lake,
Do not reflect the machine
Flying north to bomb the enemy.

Your mother vows she'll raise you in luxury after the war,
But when is the war going to end,
And how long, my baby daughter,
Will you be happy with just your simplest needs met?

When the war is over
You won't be a baby any more.
When we return to our house in Seoul,
You won't recognize the place of your birth.

My baby daughter,
Where is your hometown and your fatherland?
Will there be someone alive to tell you
When you're old enough to know?

Pak Pong-u

■

Blooming on the Wasteland

It's been long
Since we've been living
Divided into South and North.

The azaleas
Are sad,
Blooming on rusted rails.

Some have died
Calling for unification,
But history seems unmoved.

When are we going to meet
And live together?
Our Fatherland is ailing.

We
Meet
Today

To cry for
Hometown, liberty and peace,
With desperate yearning.
I in the South
You in the North
With hearts cut in two,
We suffer each other's sorrow.

Butterflies
Can fly over barbed wire fences.
When will this barrier between us
Be razed,
And by whom?

We are one race
And one nation.
The day we embrace
And sing together,
The azaleas blooming on rusted rails
Will smile with glee.

Then, on the grave of my Fatherland
History will revive, like mist in spring,
And we will not regret
Having lived through this privation.

The Window

The window doesn't open. It won't open. Then draw the white curtains aside. Won't you listen to the story of the '50s, which erupts like volcanic lava on a sterile land? Won't you listen to the stories of ordeal, of crossing mountain ranges and rivers, and walking on roads of thorn?

The window doesn't open. It won't open. Then draw the white curtains aside. Won't you listen to the sad music and the tales of those whose youth flowered in victory on a bleak field razed by blinding crossfire and the memories of survival through war?

The window doesn't open. It won't open. Then draw the white curtains aside. Haven't you heard about the people who cried uncontrollably, unable to release the bird imprisoned in the iron cage of their hearts on a June day when roses bloomed and tanks rode through a sea of blood?

The window doesn't open. It won't open. Then draw the white curtains aside. We turn ashen gray trying to find our sea on the armistice line and in the riots in Algeria and in the battle of Gaza. Won't you plant the last cries of the war dead in a flowerpot, remembering the United Nations?

The window doesn't open. It won't open. Then draw the white curtains aside. Today, the world is mirthful, disregarding Stephen Spender's 1945 poem on Deutscheland, and the bloody scenes and sad, sad, dirges created by the Korean War. Won't you listen to my discourses on the poetry of humanism growing out of my fierce battle with myself, the dreams and love babbled to a mother precious to me as my very life in this dark and stifling season?

The window doesn't open. It won't open. Then draw the white curtains aside. Won't you listen to our numbing tale of the '50s, of how we yearn for the recovery of our land even though we might end up a bloody mess on an execution ground? Of how we want to tear down and wreck the walls and wire fences dividing us on this desert island so that innumerable flowers will bloom, butterflies dancing over them, and new foliage will shoot back the noonday sun?

Half-Moon

My face
Is like the map
Of my scarred country.

It cannot wax full,
This moon
That remains split.

Perhaps one day, maybe once...

We'll shed
All our garments
For our full moon

And gather
Like dancing butterflies
That day.

My face is like
The map
Of my scarred country.

A flower blooms, growing precariously in a space rife with dark hostility, between mountains confronting each other with distrust and faces staring at each other suspiciously, knowing that the volcano is preparing to heave and rip open the earth.

The cold mutual stare shot across the armistice line. From this beautiful landscape the dauntless spirit of Koguryo and the beautiful legends of Shilla fled long ago. But the home of the stars remains one sky. Is it here that we find the meaning of our uneasy looks?

All the bloodshed has disappeared like a bad dream, but not even trees rest easy on this square. The vein remains torn. Is this repose or only a shrivelling story?

You, loathsome wind which will one day roll us up like the tongue of a venomous snake! Do you mean for us to live through that atrocious winter again? How much longer do those innocent flowers have to bear this climate? Is this the only way of attaining beauty?

A flower blooms, growing precariously in a space rife with dark hostility, between mountains confronting each other with distrust and faces staring at each other suspiciously, knowing that the volcano is preparing to heave and rip open the earth.

Pak Yang-kyun

■

Flower

"God will answer you with silence."
—Rilke

At whose request have you bloomed on this wasteland where men slaughtered men, you nameless flower that confronts the sky with your fragile sweetness? How can you, a delicate plant standing upon your frail stalk on a sunny road beneath blue heaven, efface, with your ineffable smile, the deafening din of cannons and bombs, and the screams and bloodbaths that shook the earth to its core?

Yi Hyo-sang
■

Fatherland

I lost my fatherland when young
And had to call a usurper my liege.
Those thirty-six years left
A bitter resentment in my heart.

Providence was not blind, and with the help of brave patriots
We regained sovereignty in 1945.
Oh, how tears flooded my cheeks
As we waved our national flag!

Was it through somebody's malevolence or heaven's plan
That the country was divided at the 38th Parallel?
My body is weak and ailing.
Will I live to see my fatherland free and whole?

Instead of union, war broke out
And we were trampled by red devils.
My hapless compatriots fled loaded with bundles.
Now, what further misfortune awaits my fatherland?

But,
I never loved my fatherland as dearly as now.
I didn't know one's fatherland was such a precious thing.
I realize for the first time that my life is a mere feather weighed
        against my fatherland.
I realize belatedly that your fatherland is something
You embrace with death looking over your shoulder.

War

Every time unbearable fury rose in me
War seemed a little closer to me.

At last came the day I sent my beloved son to the army
And his younger brother sat on the verandah with a sad face.
Then war entered my heart.

That day I felt so ashamed.
For the past two months I'd been acting the great patriot.
When neighbors scurried to escape the war I remained calm
And I could regard the endless stream of refuges without tears
Because my faith in our victory was strong.

The day I sent my servants, nephews, cousins on Mother's side,
Cousins on Father's side, and a hundred youths from the village
          to the war,
I made a moving speech, with words welling up from my heart.
But the day I sent my son, the thought that I was a hypocrite
Smote my conscience.

The day I sent my beloved son to the war
I wished I could fight in his place.
I had wanted to live without sin and lies,
And was resolved to shatter like a quartz stone
If I came up against a rock.
But I tossed and turned all night, hugging my fatherland in my
          arms.
War came, at last, into my hand.

Yi Yong-Sang

■

The Day You Tearfully Embrace Our Fatherland

*after meeting a wounded sixteen-year-old People's Army
prisoner of war in an army hospital*

White clouds hover lightly on pomgranate boughs outside the
    window
And soft sunshine fills this hospital room
Where a boy is crying for his mother!
He is a soldier of the People's Army captured in the battle of
    Yŏngch'ŏn.
His surname is Yi and given name is Yŏng-sŏk.
Hoeryŏng is his hometown, and he is sixteen years of age.
He said he could not bid his mother goodbye when he left,
    that airplanes scared him, and he was hungry.

Poor boy, warrior of the People's Army.
You must have sung the military songs and marches
And tried to keep in step with the others
When you left your hometown, deceived by their sweet propaganda.
So, what came of your zeal to drive the entire Republic's Army into
    the sea
And capture Pusan in a whirlwind campaign?
You are asking me, your enemy yesterday, for cookies,
You sixteen-year-old prisoner of war!
Yes, I'll buy you cookies.
I, your compatriot and a soldier of the Korean Republic.

Poor boy, warrior of the People's Army!
Don't cry out for your mother in your pain
But let the bosom of your fatherland heal you!
When you realize, with your innocent, cookie-craving heart,
How wrong it was to join the People's Army,
You'll cry in gratitude for our Fatherland
And for liberty.

I Can Love a North Korean

to Sergeant Richard who gave burial to an enemy soldier
and prayed before the grave

When you gathered the corpse of a dead enemy
On this savage battlefield,
Buried him in the evening sun, and planted a cross on the grave,
You looked to me like one of those holy rustics
In Jean Francois Millet's painting.

How you must have hated North Koreans
When you crossed the stormy ocean
To come to this faraway foreign land,
Leaving behind all those you love!
You must have wanted to incinerate them all.

But you said,
I love North Koreans;
I only hate Communists,
As you buried an enemy's corpse
And prayed over the cross you planted on his grave.
When your shadow fell on the earth with that of the cross
In the savage battlefield lit by the evening sun,
In your heart rang
The bells of your chapel
In your faraway home
And the war between democracy and communism disappeared;
You yearned for peace on earth and peace for mankind
As you would for the morning star on a dark night.

"I love North Koreans.
I only hate Communism."
I recited these words of yours over and over
And wiped hot tears from my cheeks,

Thinking of you
Singing Hallelujah
Bending over an enemy's grave.

Yi Tŏk-chin

■

The Ridge of Blood

I am looking at a scene of slaughter now.
Earth and sky alike swoon
At the deafening roar of cannon.
But the dove-white 1211 Height
Is resplendent in the rising sun.

How cavalier is the moment that separates
The living from the dead!
Flesh bursts and blood spurts,
And streams of crimson dye the surrounding valleys red.
The landscape changes as corpses pile up,
And the ridge becomes a bloodthirsty devil.

After the birth of a bloody and solemn legend
That will be told for ten thousand years,
The battlefield is like primitive earth.
The soldier shoulders his valiant fallen comrade.

Yi Yun-su
■

The Foot Soldier Marches

We're marching.
We're marching on foot.
We march onward and onward
Day and night in search of the enemy.
We march everywhere,
We march in silence.
We march, bathed in sweat,
Our bodies sizzling in the sun.
We march along endless dusty country roads.
We wade through rivers if bridges are destroyed.
We push through like tanks on roads tanks can't run.
We march with iron will and high spirit.
We march through rain, clasping guns whose straps dig into
        our shoulders.
We march through mud,
We march over felled trees,
And navigate through forests.

We march.
We march on foot.
We keep marching forward and forward.
Day and night we march in search of the enemy.
We march anywhere,
We march in silence.

We march, soothing little children of our hometown
Who cling to our unshaven beards.
We march, carrying locks of dead comrades' hair in our bosom.
We march North, all the way up to the horizon.
We march in search of a sunny place to bury our comrades' locks
        of hair.
We march, carrying the glory of our only Fatherland.
We keep marching come what may.

We march, munching on pine needles to allay our hunger,
And drinking the water in flooded paddies to slake our thirst.

We march.
We march on foot.
We march onward and onward
Day and night we march in search of the enemy.
We march everywhere,
We march in silence.

We march through icy blizzards of the North.
We march through snow and more snow.
We march over the battle front, over which summer and autumn
        have passed, through piles of snow.
We march over the hilly terrain of the North
Walking over hills, more hills and still more hills.
We march until the soles of our boots feel like red-hot iron.
We can go everywhere, we go everywhere.
When we can't walk, we crawl.
Nothing can stop us now.

We march, we march on foot.
Behold! Our feet can march forever!
Day and night, through fire and flood,
We march onward in search of the enemy.
We march come what may.

The Northern Front

To a Supply Unit

Snow is falling silently on the thousand-*li* northern front.
Huge flakes of snow fall on the thousand-*li* expanse of
      powder smoke and cannon roar.
I walk through the snow with a comrade, like a leopard.
I walk through the snow leading a war horse, on land where there
      is no road.

The crimson spots of blood on the snow must have been
      spilled by a wounded comrade.
It looks like if I touched them, I could feel their warmth.

In the mountain gorge where there is no road, red blossoms of
      blood on snow!
My fury grows, walking through gorgeous flowers of blood.

Following the string of gorgeous petals
I walk through endless mountains, endless snow.

Yu Chong

■

Envy

Inside the double cage of this mental hospital
Beside a street strewn with yellow flowers
And crimson buds here and there
Making it look as gorgeous
As a distant mountain valley covered with morning clouds,
I have difficulty breathing
Looking at an old comrade
Who doesn't recognize me
And raves on.
His black eyes vacantly stare,
And when his youthful-looking wife
Drops her head
To hide a shining streak on her cheek,
A bolt
Of something resembling envy
Runs down my back,
And I, a handicapped veteran,
Vault up and leave,
Pulling my hat over my forehead.

Walking the street
Where petals are blowing like a blizzard,
I wish we were back on the battlefield
Where we could not tell whether we were alive or dead.

Brothers

Aren't you my second brother who left our hometown of apricot
        blossoms with our bull
And were said to be roaming China?
"I came back to die.
Will Father forgive me?"

Brother! My brother!
Standing on one leg like a grasshopper,
In tattered quilted trousers of the People's Army,
Your sunken eyes under blood-clotted forehead
Gleam with emotion.

Those emaciated shoulders heaving in pitch darkness
I glimpsed while peering across the frozen 38th Parallel
Stretching with an icy gleam in utter silence—
They are my brother's, without a doubt.

Father isn't alive any more.
Even Mother and sister, who called us desperately with pallid faces,
Disappeared into the powder smoke one morning
Together with our hometown covered with apricot blossoms.

In this accursed age
Blood kin, who parted as enemies,
Now see each other only as spectres
That may be either dead or alive.

Are you lying in a mountain cave tonight,
While I'm lying in a trench in a minefield?
In the sky we both look up at from our separate holes
The stars are so clear and bright
Their icy light freezes the earth.

Syngman Rhee
■

At *Pulguksa Temple*

My heart is full on beholding the Pulguksa Temple
Whose name I heard so often when young.
The mute hills brood silently on the history of old kingdoms
But the whispering brooks prattle tales from the past.
Spring grasses grow all around the Half Moon Wall,
And wildflowers bloom under the Ch'ŏmsŏngdae Tower.
Today, dust of battle has settled everywhere,
And soldiers are resting in the breeze stirring the pines on the
    ancient battlement.

Swallow

The swallow, returned from the South,
Cries that its nest is gone and only cold ashes remain.
Swallow, there's no one to heed your thousand words
       of complaint.
None in this time of war is without a grief of his own.

On the Road Between Chinhae and Pusan

*Written upon beholding young and old women
heading toward a fair at Naktong River.*

The daughter-in-law carrying a fish basket and the mother-in-law
     leading a cow
Are heading toward the ten-*li* long fair along the Naktong River.
Woodcutter husbands and fisherman sons are all at the scene of
     slaughter:
The whole country is still at war.

Spring in Wartime

The whole peninsula is wrapped in battle smoke,
And Chinese flags and the sails of Western ships hide the spring
       sky.
All who come and go are homeless vagabonds,
And they are all fasting, like gods that shun food.
Of the citadel only the ancient walls remain,
And farmers are burning forests to make farmland.
The spring wind does not wait for the war to cease,
And new grass is sprouting all around the ruined citadel.

At Pusan, in the spring of 1951

A Casual Verse

*Written in lament of the Chinese Communists
entering the war on the North Korean side.*

We, thirty million Koreans
And you, four hundred million Chinese
How have we come to slaughter each other?
Are we determined to be each other's enemy?

Early spring of 1952

At Haein Temple

This is Haeinsa, the most famous temple east of China.
Its nest, the Kaya Mountain, is as lusciously green as ever.
The pavilion sits on infinitely spreading jade mist,
And monks lie couched on shimmering white clouds.
Under the Lonely Cloud Bower stands a thousand-year-old tree,
And into the Hall of Eternal Silence blows ceaseless wind.
The monks say it is all owing to Buddha's grace
That the eighty thousand scripture blocks escaped harm from the
      war.

At the Ch'onggan Pavillion in Kansong

I am standing at the eastern edge of the peninsula.
All the hills in sight look like the divine peaks of legend.
Wasn't it here that youths sent by Shi Huang Ti looked for the
        elixir of life?
And when was it that Emperor Wu of Han China dreamed of this
        bower?
Aren't those the green hills of Yaemaek outside the gate?
And isn't the crimson sun rising above the terrace the sun of
        Puyo?
Amidst the war no one claims this superb landscape.
It is left to fishermen and white gulls.

Notes on the Poems

Page 39 - North Korea crossed the 38th parallel to launch an attack on the South on the 25th of June, 1950, but most of the civilians did not take refuge immediately because the government of Syngman Rhee assured the people that the North Koreans would be repelled quickly and that the government would stay in Seoul with the people.

Page 43 - Wonhyoro is located on the north shore of the Han River.

Page 45 - Contrary to its repeated promises, the government of South Korea exploded the bridges on the Han River at dawn of the 28th of June, to hinder the Communist forces advancing further south but thereby cutting off the civilians' escape route at the same time.

Deploying the forces between the river and the enemy, so that the soldiers would put up a desperate fight, knowing that death by drowning is the only alternative to beating off the enemy, is one of the classical strategies in Chinese books on the art of war and utilized with brilliant success by many renowned generals in Chinese and Korean history. The irony here is that it is innocent and trusting civilians thus hemmed in between two deadly alternatives.

Mapo, Sŏbinggo, and Kwangnaru are the names of districts along the northern shore of the Han River.

Page 46 - In the Korean poetic convention, "beloved" often implies an object of one's absolute worship and loyalty, such as one's king, country, nation, or the ideals of justice and righteousness.

Page 51 - Ch'ŏngma is the penname of Yu Ch'i-hwan, represented in this collection

Taegu is the third largest city in South Korea.

Seoul, which fell to the communists on the 28th of June, three days after the Communists launched their attack, was recaptured on September 28 by General Douglas MacArthur, who had successfully maneuvered a surprise landing at Inchon on the 15th of September. So, people who had taken refuge returned to Seoul.

Page 58 - During the three-months-long Communist occupation of Seoul, many prominent figures who failed to flee were imprisoned, tortured and killed and more were abducted to the North at the time of the Communists' retreat.

Often, at times of famine, Koreans ate grass, roots, tree bark, and acorns. Acorns contain an ingredient which causes poisoning in many people.

Page 61 - This is not a reference to a secret lover. In Korean literature, especially in poetry, there is a tradition of addressing or referring to one's country, nation, or king as "beloved," as an object of worship and devotion.

Page 65 - *Nalnari* is a rather shrill wind instrument, which is a staple of the farmers' band.

Page 66 - Chongro is one of the two main streets in Seoul, running from east to west. It has been a major artery of Seoul since Chosŏn Dynasty times, and a center of business and commerce.

After the recapture of Seoul on the 28th of September, the U.N. and South Korean forces kept pushing the Communists North, all the way to the border with China. But with the People's Republic of China joining the war on the North Korean side with 500,000 forces in late October, the war situation took a drastic turn, the combined U.N. and ROK forces had to retreat south, and Seoul was briefly occupied by Communists once more, early in 1951.

There is a famous bell and a bell pavilion in the Chongro main intersection. The bell dates back to 1395, the fourth year of the Chosŏn Dynasty, and has been used to signal the hours for opening and closing of the city gates. The pavilion was burnt during the 16th century Japanese invasion and was later rebuilt. It was burnt again during the Korean War and rebuilt again. Since the founding of the republic, the bell has been struck thirty-three times every New Year's Eve by the Seoul city mayor and other dignitaries to ring in the new year.

Korean bells are rung not by shaking them and thereby making the clapper hit the sides but by striking them from the outside, usually with the end of a great log thrust at it horizontally, thus creating vibration. (Korean bells have no clappers and weigh many tons.) The sound, therefore, is not high-pitched and gay, but deep and resonant.

Page 77 - The Diamond Mountain is a mountain sacred to Koreans for its scenic beauty and otherworldly atmosphere. It is located in North Korea, but in the autumn of 1998 it was opened for South Korean tourists.

Page 82 - Having been collectively poor more or less throughout history, most Koreans, when seated at a feast, or even given a square meal, would think of their family members who would relish the food.

Page 85 - Li is a Korean measure of distance. One li is roughly equivalent to a quarter of a mile.

Page 90 - Koreans offer food and spirits to the ghosts of their dead ancestors on the anniversaries of their deaths and on New Year's and Harvest Festival days.

Page 91 - This is a reference to the 1656 wreck of the Dutch ship on the seas near Cheju Island, which left thirty-three of the ship's crew stranded on the shore of the island. Of the thirty-three, seven men later escaped to Japan and eventually to the Netherlands. Hendrik Hamel, one of the seven, wrote an account of the shipwreck and his residence in Korea, which gave the West their first view of Korea. In the early days of their residence in Korea, the Dutchmen were made to contribute their knowledge toward making firearms, etc.: hence the allusion here to bringing civilization to Korea.

Page 108 - Most Korean women still wore traditional Korean dresses at the time of the Korean War.

Page 110 - Sim Ch'ŏng is the lengendary filial daughter who sold herself to sailors as a human sacrifice to be offered to the malicious sea-god, in return for three hundred bags of rice, which her blind father foolishly pledged to the monk who promised him sight. Moved by her filial piety, the Dragon King, the good sea-god, sent her back to earth inside a gigantic lotus blossom. A fisherman found the blossom and offered it to the king. The king, finding Sim Ch'ŏng in the blossom, made her his queen. As Queen, Sim Ch'ŏng throws a feast for all the blind men in the realm. At the feast, hearing his presumably dead daughter call to him, Sim Ch'ŏng's father recovers his sight from astonishment.

Panmumjŏm was the site the armistice talks were held, and it is still the site of almost all North-South talks.

Page 129 - DPRK: Democratic People's Republic of Korea is the formal name of North Korea

KATUSA: Korean Auxiliary Troop to the U. S. Army

Page 131 - Mt. Chiri is the mountain where most Communists and their sympathizers fled before and during the Korean War to escape the Republic of Korea's police and military forces and which became the base of their guerrilla warfare.

Page 135 - Taehan means Great Han, or the Great Country of the Han race, Han being the comprehensive racial name of the Korean people. Yi Sun-shin is the great admiral who decimated the Japanese naval forces during the 16th century Japanese invasion, commonly known as the Hideyoshi Invasion.

Tangun is the legendary founder of ancient Korea. He is the son of the heavenly emperor's son Hwanung and a bear who became a woman after successfully withstanding a trial of patience for a hundred days in a dark cave. Tradition has it that Tangun founded the ancient Chosŏn in 2333 B.C.

Page 141 - Flower Youths were youths rigorously and vigorously trained to be warriors and gentlemen in the Shilla dynasty (57 B.C.–A.D. 935).

Page 143 - Ch'ŏnji Lake is the lake filling the huge crater on top of the Paekdu (White Head) mountain, which is the highest mountain in Korea and which is located on the northern border of Korea; hence, drinking a sip of the water from the Ch'ŏnji Lake signifies the wish to see the country unified.

Page 148 - The hills and mountains of Korea were deforested by the Japanese for timber during the occupation years and by Koreans for fuel wood during the penurious years after liberation.

Page 159 - Hamkyŏng-do is the name of the northernmost province in North Korea
   Mt. Chiri is a mountain in the southern part of South Korea.
   Mt. Halla is the volcanic mountain in the center of Cheju Island on the southern tip of south Korea.
   Mt. Paekdu, Kŭmkang, and the Kaema heights are famous natural attractions in North Korea.
   Three thousand li is the measure of the entire Korean peninsula from the northern to the southern tip.

Page 167 - White Horse Hill is where a series of fierce and deadly battles were fought during the Korean War.
Page 183 - Before modern theories and methods of child rearing were introduced in Korea, Korean mothers used to suckle their

babies for up to two or three years, with supplementary diets after the first year. This practice is usually credited with giving the babies emotional stability.

Page 187 - The rusted rails here refer to the railroad running from the South to the North, which stopped operating shortly after the division of the country.

Page 199 - Actually, the years of subjugation under the Japanese colonial rule were from 1910 to 1945, hence thirty-five years instead of thirty-six, but the traditional Korean way of counting time counts the initial year (or day, month, etc.) as one, and add each subsequent unit to that, so those years are always numbered as thirty-six.

Page 227 - China and Korea had enjoyed an amicable, fraternal relationship for over a thousand years prior to this.

Page 228 - President Rhee visited Haeinsa Temple with U. S. Ambassador to Korea Ellis O. and Mrs. Briggs, U. S. Ambassador to the Soviet Union William C. Bullitt, General Maxwell Taylor, and several friends.

Lonely Cloud Bower was named after Ch'oe Ch'i-won (857-?), the famous scholar of the Late Silla period, whose pen name was Ko-un, or Lonely Cloud.

The Tripitaka Koreana, or the eighty thousand (actually 81,137) wooden printing blocks for Buddhist scriptures, were carved during the 13th century Yuan (Mongol) invasion, and embody the Korean nation's prayer to Buddha to protect the country from the invaders. The blocks are housed in a special warehouse in Haeinsa and are among the UNESCO-designated world's cultural heritage.

Page 229 - Yaemaek and Puyo are ancient kingdoms (or tribal states) that existed in prehistoric Korea, on the territory north of the Yalu River which is part of Manchuria now but used to be part of Korea until the fall of Koguryo in the seventh century.

OTHER KOREAN VOICES FROM WHITE PINE PRESS

SHRAPNEL AND OTHER STORIES:
SELECTED STORIES OF DONG-HA LEE
Edited by Hyun-jae Yee Sallee
Translated by Hyun-jae Yee Sallee and Elaine LaMattina
1-893996-53-0   176 pages $16.00 paperback

AMONG THE FLOWERING REEDS:
CLASSIC KOREAN POEMS WRITTEN IN CHINESE
Edited and Translated by Kim Jong-gil
1-89396-54-9   176 pages $16.00 paperback

A SKETCH OF THE FADING SUN:
STORIES OF WAN-SUH PARK
Edited and translated by Hyun-jae Yee Sallee
1-877727-93-8   200 pages $15.00 paperback

THE SNOWY ROAD:
AN ANTHOLOGY OF KOREAN FICTION
Edited and translated by Hyun-jae Yee Sallee
1-877727-19-9   168 pages $12.00 paperback

HEART'S AGONY:
SELECTED POEMS OF CHI-HA KIM
Translated by Won-chun Kim and James Han
1-8777237-84-9   128 pages $14.00 paperback

STRONG WIND AT MISHI PASS:
POEMS BY TONG-GYU HWANG
Translated by Seong-kon Kim and Dennis Maloney
1-893996-10-7   118 pages $15.00 paperback